☝ **W9-BKG-903**

TOPICS IN AUTISM

SECOND EDITION

Functional Behavior Assessment for People with Autism

MAKING SENSE OF SEEMINGLY SENSELESS BEHAVIOR

Beth A. Glasberg, Ph.D., BCBA-D & Robert H. LaRue, Ph.D., BCBA-D

Sandra L. Harris, Ph.D., series editor

Woodbine House

Library of Congress Cataloging-in-Publication Data

Glasberg, Beth A.
  Functional behavior assessment for people with autism : making sense of seemingly senseless behavior / Beth A. Glasberg and Robert H. LaRue. -- Second edition.
     pages cm
  Includes bibliographical references and index.
  ISBN 978-1-60613-204-3 (pbk.)
  1. Autism. 2. Autism in children. 3. Behavioral assessment. 4. Behavioral assessment of children. 5. Behavior disorders in children--Diagnosis. I. LaRue, Robert H. II. Title.
  RC553.A88G63 2015
  616.85'882--dc23
                                                              2014046172

Manufactured in the United States of America

10   9   8   7   6   5   4   3   2   1

This book is for all of the parents and teachers who have broken a few rules—like giving that cookie to a child when he didn't ask exactly as expected, laughing at a wisecrack when they meant to keep a straight face, and offering a hug here and there when it wasn't quite the right time. Forget perfection: we salute parents and teachers who are out there every day doing their best.

And for our families for giving us the love and support we need to accomplish our goals. We could not have completed this book without them!

Table of Contents

Introduction

Is This Your Child?

Does your child engage in a behavior that just doesn't seem to make any sense? For example, does his behavior hurt or disturb others, or appear to go against what your child wants for himself? Has your child been punished for the behavior, yet he keeps on doing it? Would you just give him what he seems to want if only he would use his words? As a parent or teacher of someone displaying these seemingly senseless behaviors, you might find yourself feeling frustrated and confused. You are not alone. Unfortunately, these perplexing behaviors are fairly common among individuals with autism spectrum disorders (ASD). Take a look at the four stories below and see if any of them sound like your story.

Grace Carmichael

By October, Ms. Brandt was ready to quit her job. While she had thoroughly enjoyed teaching her second grade class for the last several years, this year was different. Little Grace Carmichael was ruining her life. Grace was an eight-year-old girl with ASD who was included in Ms. Brandt's regular education classroom. Grace was very interested in other children and repeatedly told her mother how excited she was to be in her new classroom and to make friends. Grace might go days with no problems at all, and then suddenly, she might stand up, pick up her chair, and smash it on the foot of the child seated next to her. While doing a crafts activity, she might bite the arm of a student working with her. While standing in line, she might slap the child in front of her.

Grace's victims would yell at her or try to hit her back, but Grace persisted in her aggressive behavior. Grace had been sent to the principal's office, lost her dessert at lunchtime, and had her mother called to come and pick her up—all to no avail; the behaviors persisted. Ms. Brandt wanted to help Grace, but she had virtually no experience with special education or behavior problems. The school psychologist had never worked with behavior problems this inconsistent or severe. Although Grace was making progress in her academics, socially her classroom placement was a failure. The other children had become afraid of her. Ms. Brandt hesitated to ask for Grace to be placed in a more restrictive setting because she felt that Grace had the potential to benefit from the inclusive setting, but she believed that these dangerous and disruptive behaviors were leaving her no choice.

Jamaal Brown

Four-year-old Jamaal Brown had been doing very well in his home-based discrete trial instruction program. In fact, his parents and teachers were starting to eye the inclusive kindergarten classroom as a possible placement for the upcoming school year. Not only was he flying through his academic, self-help, and motor programs, but his social skills programming was also going swimmingly. He could have entire conversations about various topics while using appropriate body language and intonation.

His parents and teachers were sure he was ready for typically developing peers, and enrolled Jamaal in a children's gymnastics class to see how he would do. Much to their surprise, Jamaal did not interact well with the other children. Although he watched them closely and seemed interested in their activities, he did not go near them. When peers approached him, Jamaal would look right at them while making a strange face and adopting a crooked posture with his body. Sadly, the other children quickly stopped trying to play with Jamaal.

Darra Littman

If Darra Littman's mother had told her once, she had told her a thousand times: no more discussion of the boy band One Direction (One-D). Darra had seen One-D on television and hadn't stopped talking about them since. At first, Darra's parents were excited—finally, their daughter with high functioning ASD was interested in an age-appropriate icon. The embarrassment of having a preteen who adored Sesame Street characters was at last at an end. And her peers noticed! They were very impressed with Darra's knowledge of all things "One-D."

Unfortunately, Darra's interest in One-D continued to mushroom. She began to turn almost any conversation in the band's direction, no matter how unrelated. These odd changes of topic made her peers uncomfortable and eventually resulted in them avoiding her. Nevertheless, Darra's focus on One-D intensified. She could discuss nothing else. At this point, her mother decided to end the obsessive talk. She forbade any discussion of One-D. Furthermore, she made a rule that any mention of the group would cost Darra ten minutes of evening television time, which she treasured. Nevertheless, the "One-D" talk persisted. Last night, Darra lost all two hours of her allotted television time in the evening. The strange part was, this had no discernible impact on the "One-D" talk. Mrs. Littman could not understand why this behavior was so out of control.

Anthony Cappozolli

Mr. Cappozolli heard that familiar, unwelcome sound in the living room and went running. Just as he'd expected, he found Anthony, his nonverbal, fifteen-year-old son with ASD, banging his head against the windowpane. "Anthony!" he yelled, pulling him away. He sternly reminded him that head banging is dangerous and not allowed. Mr. Cappozolli then led Anthony over to a box of beads, off limits at other times, that the family used to distract him from continuing this perilous behavior.

Today, the Cappozollis were lucky—Anthony hadn't broken the glass. Other times, they had not been so lucky. This behavior had cost them numerous trips to the emergency room and numerous windowpanes. More importantly, it had cost Anthony's parents an untold amount of worry and grief, and had given them a sickening sense that they were helpless to protect their own son from himself. While grateful that he and his wife had the beads to interrupt the head banging, Mr. Cappozolli wished that he could understand where the head banging came from, and ultimately prevent it altogether.

The four children described above illustrate just a few of the behavior problems that children with an autism spectrum disorder may display. Your child may be challenging you with noncompliance, inattention, repetitive behaviors, or other problems. Some behaviors may be life-threatening, while others are just plain irritating. Some behaviors may lead to the destruction of property, while others may lead to the destruction of relationships with family or friends. For some parents, these behaviors are a constant, painful reminder of their child's disability. For others, they may be a constant barrier to getting their child into the community and participating in the world.

While each type of behavior appears very different from the others, they do share a common thread. Each of the above behaviors does not seem to make any sense. The children engaging in these behaviors are losing things they value, ranging from television time to positive interactions with peers, but they are engaging in the behaviors anyway. Some behaviors, such as Anthony's head banging, appear to be enormously painful, yet the behaviors persist.

For those who care about these children and desperately want them to be safe, happy individuals with a rich circle of friends and loved ones, these behaviors are enormously frustrating and are often the barriers between where these children are and where we want them to be. The purpose of this book is to help tear down these barriers. This book will help readers to identify how and why these troubling behaviors arise as well as to learn the basics of a strategy to eliminate them. Additionally, while this book cannot help with certain behaviors that require medication (such as tics), it can help you learn to distinguish behaviors that are part of underlying medical issues from those that will respond to behavioral intervention.

Over the years, research and experience have taught professionals who study behavior that making sense of a seemingly senseless behavior is an essential step to controlling it. This means that we must accept that these behaviors make perfect sense to the individuals engaging in them and then identify why. We must ask ourselves, "What purpose is this behavior serving?" and "How is this behavior benefiting my child?"

Well-established procedures have been developed to systematically identify the factors contributing to the occurrence of behavior problems in people with disabilities. Collectively, these procedures are referred to as "functional behavior assessment." Results of functional behavior assessments are then ideally used to develop effective behavior intervention plans.

Study after study has shown that relying on a thorough functional behavior assessment is the most likely way to succeed in addressing an unwanted behavior (e.g., Repp, Felce & Barton, 1988). Behavior intervention plans based on functional behavior assessments work for individuals of all ages and all functioning levels (e.g., Crone, Hawken & Bergstrom, 2007; McLaren & Nelson, 2009; Wilder et al., 2009). This approach is relevant for individuals with the most severe developmental delays as well as for typically developing children and adults with no diagnosis at all. The research behind functional behavior assessment is so compelling that, legally, public schools in the United States *must* consider completing this type of assessment when addressing challenging behaviors (Individuals with Disabilities Education Act, 2004).

You do not have to be an expert in behavior analysis to understand and implement a functional behavior assessment. This book will teach readers how to complete comprehensive functional behavior assessments independently. In addition, this revised edition includes strategies that have been developed since the publication of our first edition that make it far easier to use these principles in home and school settings. The book has been written to help parents, grandparents, group home staff, and other caregivers, as well as teachers, school psychologists, and other professionals who may not have had access to specific training in this area. The methods described in this book can be used with toddlers, preschoolers, school-aged children, adolescents, and adults with any type of autism spectrum disorder, as well as other individuals with problem behaviors.

A general introduction to the principles of behavior will be provided in Chapters 1 and 2, including a discussion of how challenging behaviors arise and why individuals with autism spectrum disorders are more susceptible to developing them. Other foundation topics covered in these chapters will include an introduction to the principles of learning, a discussion of factors determining which behaviors will be performed in a given situation, and an overview of the types of consequences that may strengthen behaviors. Furthermore, Chapters 1 and 2 include an overview of functional behavior assessment and a discussion of how functional behavior assessment helps make sense of otherwise perplexing behaviors.

This background will equip readers for Chapters 3 through 8, which offer a practical, step-by-step guide to completing a functional assessment, including various forms of functional analysis—the "gold standard" in identifying the reasons why a behavior is occurring and informing effective intervention. These chapters also include "Keep it

Simple Tips" to make the process more manageable, and handy tools to use when completing an assessment. This guide will help readers learn how to interpret assessment results, which are ultimately needed to develop an effective intervention. Chapter 9 summarizes the process, while Chapter 10 provides an overview of how to turn these assessment results into an effective plan. Finally, Chapter 11 addresses special topics such as adult issues, very infrequent but severe behaviors, and troubleshooting.

Armed with this combination of knowledge and skills, readers will be ready to make sense of those seemingly senseless behaviors and help their children or students tear down barriers to leading fuller and happier lives. If someone you care about is being held back by interfering behaviors, you can gain the skills to make a difference in his or her life. To begin empowering yourself to help, read on.

1 | Why Problem Behaviors Occur

B ehavior problems can be maddening. Think about the examples described in the Introduction. Why would Anthony inflict so much pain on himself? Why would Grace destroy her chances of friendship with such violent behaviors? The answers to these questions are just not obvious. Professionals have struggled to understand behavior problems for a very long time. This chapter will give you a quick overview of how our thinking about the causes of, and interventions for, behavior problems has changed over time, and then tie that into the current thinking about why problem behaviors occur so often in individuals with autism spectrum disorders (ASDs).

How Do We Think about Behavior Problems? A Quick History

The Punishment-Based Approach

Historically, behavior interventions did not take into account the possible causes for a behavior. Instead, they focused on the question, "What is she doing?" Based on what a behavior looked like and what body parts were involved, a punishment was chosen. For example, if a boy swore, his mother might wash his mouth out with soap. If a girl hit someone, her teacher might hold her arms down at her side for thirty seconds. Through a trial-and-error process using this strategy, caregivers looked for an effective punishment. In fact, a punishment-based approach is often the first intervention strategy that many nonprofessionals try even today.

There are numerous problems with this approach. First of all, when we use this type of punishment, we never find out what the individual has been gaining from performing the problem behavior. The fact that she did it at all tells us that she was getting something out of it. Therefore, even if our punishment works, meaning that it gets rid of the behavior, the individual still has no appropriate way to get what she wants. This makes it likely that she will find a new way to meet her need—and we may not like it any better than the old way. For example, if a boy is punished for hitting his teacher whenever he is asked to do his schoolwork, he may indeed stop hitting her, but then start swiping work materials off of his desk instead. Either behavior will have the equivalent effect of postponing his schoolwork.

Secondly, if we take action without knowing what the child has been getting out of a behavior, we may inadvertently reward it. Let's revisit the boy who was hitting his teacher. For this example, let's imagine that this behavior persisted because it helped him avoid his work. If we punish him by sending him to the principal's office (away from his work), we are inadvertently rewarding his behavior and increasing the chances that he will hit again.

A final problem with this type of punishment is that an individual may "habituate," or get used to, a certain level of punishment over time (e.g., Ratner, 1970). This requires the person doing the intervention to gradually increase the intensity of the punishment in order to maintain its effectiveness. For example, the first time that you want your son to stop poking his sister, you may be able to deter him with a stern voice. Over time, you may need to raise your voice a bit. Soon, you may find yourself actually yelling, and so on. Eventually, you may arrive at some level of punishment that you are not comfortable with. When you consider escalation of other forms of punishment, from putting something that tastes bad into a child's mouth up through spanking, you can see how the need for increased intensity becomes more and more problematic.

Time-Out

A second intervention for difficult behaviors that has historically been very popular and remains very popular is "time-out" (Ferster,

1958). There are various permutations of time-out procedures, but the most basic element of this intervention is the removal of an individual from the setting where the behavior problem occurred. For example, a student who hits in class may be removed from the classroom for a given period of time. Time-out offers an alternative to more traditional, physical forms of punishment-based discipline, such as spanking, and is firmly entrenched in current parenting culture. Stop any parent at your local playground and ask how long a time-out for a five-year-old should be. They will likely inform you, without a moment's hesitation, to use one minute for every year of the child's age. Parents and teachers everywhere have become time-out experts.

Despite time-out's celebrity, there are problems with relying on it as the solution to every behavior problem. In fact, at times, using time-out actually might encourage a child to engage in a behavior more often. For example, in 1994, Brian Iwata and his colleagues summarized their work with over 150 people with developmental disabilities who were hurting themselves, a classic example of a seemingly senseless behavior. The research revealed that almost 40 percent of the time, self-injury was occurring as a way of getting out of or away from something. Like the boy described above who hit to escape work, these individuals were hurting themselves in an effort to leave a situation. As you might imagine, if a child who engaged in self-injury was sent to time-out, then we would see a cycle in which the child is motivated to escape a situation, hurts herself, and escapes the situation.

More recently, in a sample of thirty-two children seen in an outpatient clinic for varied problem behaviors, a group of researchers (Love et. al, 2009) found that escaping a demand was the second most common motivation for misbehaving. If these children were sent to time out (escape), then we would expect more, rather than less, problem behavior in the future.

Another challenge associated with time-out is that many children require a great deal of intervention to get them to their time-out location. This intervention may take the form of repeated instructions to go to time-out, hand holding while walking to the time-out area, or more involved physical guidance. Each of these strategies is associated with a high level of attention. If a child is engaging in a problem behavior in order to get attention, time-out may actually lead to rewarding the inappropriate behavior.

Current Thinking about the Purpose of Challenging Behavior

In the 1980s, there was a shift in the field of behavioral psychology toward viewing problematic behaviors as a form of communication. To change behaviors, we now focus on the question, "What message is that behavior communicating?" rather than on what the behavior looks like. We now know that even the most seemingly senseless behaviors make sense for the person performing the behavior.

Problematic behaviors are learned in the same manner as other forms of communication: an individual who has some need identifies a behavior to get his need met. The example above illustrates this: the boy who learned that hitting his instructor resulted in the removal of his work communicated, "Take away my work, please" by hitting. Other consequences, such as getting his hands held down by his sides or getting a talking-to from the principal, do not prevent him from learning this communication. What matters for him at that moment is that he is motivated to escape his work, and, as a result of hitting or swiping materials off of the table, he does.

Research done by Ted Carr and Mark Durand (1985) was instrumental in developing this clearer understanding of behavior problems. They documented predictable relationships between problem behaviors and the individual's environment. For example, certain people would have problem behaviors only when they were receiving very little attention. Others might display their problem behaviors whenever they were given a very difficult task to do. Different individuals engaged in their problem behaviors under different conditions. The same behavior in two different individuals might be evoked by two very different sets of conditions. By demonstrating these relationships, Carr and Durand helped to teach us that what a behavior looks like tells us very little about its origin or how to treat it.

A real-life illustration of Carr and Durand's work is provided by the behaviors of two teenage boys, Andrew and Robert. Consultation was requested for each of the boys for the same reason, aggression. Andrew blocked the door whenever a one-to-one pull-out teaching session, such as speech or counseling, was ending. He then poked his teacher if she tried to leave the room. If the staff member persisted in attempting to leave, Andrew upped the ante by threatening to stab her with scissors or to hit her with a telephone. Further assessment of this behavior revealed that Andrew behaved this way in order to maintain the rich, one-to-one attention that he had access to during these supportive therapies.

Like Andrew, Robert also poked people. Whenever his siblings sat near him or walked close enough, a swat or a poke was guaranteed. However, a closer look at Robert's behavior revealed a story very different from Andrew's. Robert poked people in order to make them go away. The longer they stayed, the more forceful the poking and swatting became. As you might imagine, Robert's siblings learned very quickly to stay away from him.

A particularly exciting result of Carr and Durand's study was the finding that teaching and reinforcing an appropriate request for whatever was desired weakened the problem behaviors. For example, teaching Andrew to ask the teacher to stay longer resulted in less door-blocking, poking, or threatening with scissors. Teaching Robert to ask for time alone got rid of his poking. The success of this approach, referred to as "functional communication training," clearly demonstrates that the difficult behaviors so often displayed by individuals with autism spectrum disorders are not an automatic byproduct of the disorder, but rather are learned behaviors, open to treatment using all of the principles of learning.

Other researchers have experimented not only with conditions that might set the stage for a problem behavior, but also with conditions that they suspected might follow a problem behavior (Iwata, Dorsey, Slifer, Bauman & Richman, 1982). This research helped demonstrate that what happens before a behavior can create a motivation for something and that engaging in a problem behavior can result in obtaining what is wanted. To illustrate, consider the boy in our example above who wanted to escape his work: the teacher approaching his desk with work materials created a motivation for him to be someplace else. Hitting his teacher resulted in him being sent to the principal's office, thereby avoiding his work. The consequences of the behavior were critical to the development of the behavior problem.

Brian Iwata and his colleagues (1982) demonstrated this idea empirically. They placed people in scenarios that mimicked these supposedly naturally occurring conditions and measured the effect on their behavior. For example, they might withhold attention from a study participant while she played with toys, but then provide attention when she performed the problem behavior (self-injury). Upon the occurrence of self-injury, the experimenter would immediately return his attention to the girl in the form of social disapproval (e.g., "Don't do that; you'll hurt yourself!"). When the consequences for the behavior were presented consistently in this way, the researchers were able to reliably produce stable patterns of the problem behavior. Using this counterintuitive approach, the researchers replicated what they believed was taking place in the real world and leading to learning. Their results showed that their hypothesis was correct: the study participants were learning these problem behaviors based on their consequences.

Iwata and his colleagues also identified a special kind of behavior that is learned through internal cues and consequences. These behaviors occur because they feel good or are inherently enjoyable for the person performing them. The conditions that trigger these behaviors and the consequences that maintain them occur inside of the individual, and thus are more complex to assess or control. Everyday examples of this type of behavior might include scratching an itch or taking a pain reliever. An observer cannot see the itch or the headache, nor can she document the consequences of removal of the itch or the headache. However, these behaviors are learned based upon the same principles as externally controlled behaviors, and numerous strategies exist to help address them.

By examining patterns of what happens before and after problem behaviors, Iwata and his colleagues were able to identify a number of communicative messages that challenging behaviors might convey. In other words, they identified the purposes that these behaviors were serving for the individuals performing them. These different purposes that behaviors serve are called "functions" of behavior and are described in Chapter 2. A quest to identify the functions of different problem behaviors was born, leading to the emergence of the field we now know as "functional behavior assessment."

Why Are Problematic Behaviors So Common among Individuals with ASD?

While all people, children and adults, typically developing or disabled, may have behavior problems, they are more common among individuals with autism spectrum disorders. When you think about the specific areas of disability associated with this group of disorders, the reasons for this relationship become clear.

Difficulties with Communication Skills

First of all, individuals with autism spectrum disorders often have impairments in communication. Consider Anthony, described in the Introduction. Recall that Anthony was nonvocal. Also recall that his family distracted him from head banging with a special box of beads. In order to keep the beads exciting for Anthony, his family had made the beads off-limits for him at other times. Therefore, Anthony was repeatedly exposed to the following sequence:

1. I have no beads.
2. I bang my head.
3. I get beads.

Anthony's head banging brings beads into his environment. Since Anthony lacks the communication skills to ask for the beads, he may have learned that banging his head is the best way for him to communicate a request for them. Even if he could request them some other way, they are off limits to him unless he is banging his head.

In a similar scenario, a colleague worked with one nonverbal student who engaged in aggressive behaviors so severe that numerous staff who worked with him had required medical attention for problems as serious as a broken nose. For safety reasons, each time he became aggressive, he was restrained in a cushiony restraint on a soft mat. A functional behavior assessment revealed that his aggressive behaviors were actually his way of requesting access to this restraint. To reduce his aggression, he was given a picture card that he could use to request the restraint. Once he mastered this communication, his aggressive behaviors virtually disappeared.

This is not to say that individuals with ASDs who can speak or sign are immune from exhibiting problem behaviors. Some people can communicate but doing so is so challenging that a problem behavior is simpler. For example, a child with communicative challenges who would like a break from her class work faces two options: 1) Identify a cue from the teacher that it is okay to raise your hand, raise your hand, wait to be called on, formulate a sentence requesting a break, and wait to see whether the teacher says yes or no; or 2) Bang the materials on your desk loudly and get sent immediately to time-out. The latter behavior seems much more efficient for the child.

Difficulties with Social Skills

Individuals with autism spectrum disorders also have social skills deficits. This means they do not engage in social interaction as easily as other people. Similarly, they may not be as skilled at interpreting social responses from others. Therefore, any social reaction they evoke may be rewarding for them. Consider Grace, our second grader who was assaulting her peers. Lacking the skills to have more meaningful social interactions, Grace may settle for the yelling and hitting that her peers are doing in response to her aggression if she cannot evoke friendly responses.

I (BG) was called in to consult with teachers about a preschooler with autism who was exhibiting a similar behavior pattern. This child was a bit larger than the other students in his segregated preschool classroom and was also more interested in socializing than his classmates were. He would often try to approach them appropriately, but would get no response. He then moved on to "belly-bopping" them, bumping them roughly with his belly. Unfortunately, this inappropriate behavior was sure to get his classmates' attention. Although the attention was often in the form of crying or yelling, for the "belly-bopper," this was preferable to no response at all. Despite his behavior problem, this child was transferred to an integrated preschool classroom where the other children were more socially aware. In this setting, where the other children responded to his more appropriate initiations, his "belly-bopping" disappeared without any other specific intervention.

Challenging behaviors can also stem from a child's desire to avoid or escape social contact. Think back to Jamaal, who made odd faces or adopted strange postures whenever his peers approached him. Jamaal's behavior quickly taught the other children to leave him alone and may have been Jamaal's way of asking them to go away. Although Jamaal's educational programming likely focused upon approaching other children and extending interactions, failing to teach children how to end or avoid social interactions is a common teaching oversight. Similarly, Robert, the teenager described above who swatted and poked his siblings to get them to keep their distance, could probably benefit from instruction in social skills for getting out of interactions appropriately.

Restricted Interests

Finally, a restricted behavioral repertoire is associated with autism spectrum disorders. This means that children with ASDs have fewer areas of interest and may focus on parts of an object or activity, rather than the whole thing. This phenomenon has been described as viewing the world with a laser beam rather than a flashlight. Darra's interest in One-D, described in the Introduction, provides a good example of this keen focus. While other preteens may have a number of pop icons who consume their interest, Darra has only One-D. Additionally, other preteens often have other interests beyond pop icons, such as sports, dance, puzzles, books, etc. Darra's range of interests is not as broad.

When a child with ASD has a narrow range of interests, it is bound to lead to a variety of problems stemming from repetition. Rather than engaging in a variety of behaviors, the individual is doing the same thing over and over again. As for Darra, this hyperfocus may lead to social problems. She is like a record with the needle stuck in a groove and keeps playing the same section of music. In other individuals, this constricted focus may play out as repetitive actions, such as hand flapping or rocking, which may be stigmatizing or even dangerous. The individual, stuck in a groove, is repeating the same behavior over and over.

Finally, some individuals may pursue their interests so single-mindedly that it leads to risky behaviors or an infringement on the rights of others. Darius McCollum, a man on the spectrum who is fascinated with transportation, provides a famous example of this possibility. Darius grew up in New York City and always loved trains. He focused so intently on subways and commuter trains that he became knowledgeable enough to "steal" subway cars and busses by posing as the driver and making all of the correct stops. At the time of this writing, he has spent over eighteen years in jail from twenty-eight arrests due to these thefts. Furthermore, he reports that he has committed his crime far more often than he has been caught.

2 | How Are Behaviors Learned?

In the Introduction, we met four children—Jamaal, Darra, Grace, and Anthony— who each exhibited very different behavior problems. The commonality among their stories is that their behaviors don't seem to make any sense. If you are reading this book, you have probably also come across a perplexing behavior or two yourself.

The only way to develop an understanding of how these challenging behaviors were learned and actually do make sense is to first understand how behaviors are learned more generally. The following section will provide a tutorial on the most important aspects of learning theory to give you a foundation to rely upon when completing a functional behavior assessment. Because functional behavior assessment grows out of learning theory, this background is essential.

Beware—this will be by far the most technical section of the book. Don't let that scare you. Once you get the gist of the concepts described below, you will have a far clearer sense of behavior, which will make it significantly easier for you to manage challenging behavior in the future and will even help you to teach new skills.

Overview of Learning Theory

Learning implies that a behavior is added to an individual's repertoire in a relatively permanent way (Catania, 1998). One can learn skills, such as addition and subtraction, or behaviors, such as brushing teeth or washing hands. One might also learn problem behaviors, such as head banging or endlessly discussing One-D. If learning were a mathematical equation, it would look like this:

Motivation + Antecedent + Behavior + Consequence = Learning

In other words, learning is the sum of four variables. We will explore each of the four variables below. Although a consequence comes chronologically at the *end* of a learning sequence, the terms and concepts relevant to consequences are important to an understanding of the first three learning variables. Therefore, consequences will be discussed first.

1) Consequences

A *consequence* is what occurs as the result of a behavior. In general, a consequence can be…
1. reinforcement, or
2. punishment.

Reinforcement
Reinforcement involves consequences that strengthen behavior. To "strengthen a behavior" means to increase the likelihood that it will occur in the future, or to increase its intensity or duration in the future. Examples of reinforcement include a woman being told that a dress looks good on her, resulting in her wearing that dress very often; a child being given a quarter for cleaning his room, resulting in him cleaning it every day; or an infant discovering that his mobile will shake around if he kicks, resulting in him kicking his legs repeatedly. In these examples, specific behaviors are strengthened by their consequences.

There are two types of reinforcement procedures: positive reinforcement and negative reinforcement.

Positive Reinforcement. When "positive reinforcement" is at work, the consequence that strengthens behavior involves adding something to the individual's environment. For example, beads were added to Anthony's environment as a consequence for head banging. His parents had unintentionally delivered positive reinforcement for head banging. Positive reinforcement can involve receiving access to anything that the individual is motivated to obtain, including attention, a certain sensation, a particular activity, food, money, tokens, etc.

Some things that act as positive reinforcers don't look appealing to an outsider at all. For example, the "belly-bopper" described in Chapter 1 was getting tears and yells from peers, and this consequence was strengthening his behavior of belly-bopping. Tears and yells were acting as positive reinforcers for belly-bopping. The other student described in Chapter 1 was physically restrained with a squishy mat when he was aggressive, and this consequence was strengthening his behavior of aggression. A physical restraint was acting as positive reinforcement for aggression.

The only way to determine whether a given consequence is a reinforcer is to measure its effect on behavior. If it increases a behavior, it's a reinforcer. Remember, reinforcers don't have to look good; they just have to strengthen behavior.

Here's a quick quiz:

1. If I give my son a Skittle every time he goes pee-pee in the potty, but he is doing it less and less, have I reinforced the behavior? No, because the consequence is decreasing the behavior.
2. If I yell every time my son goes in the potty and complain loudly that now I have to clean it out, and he goes more and more in the potty, have I reinforced the behavior? Yes, because this consequence is increasing the probability of pee-pee in the potty.
3. If I give my son a star on a chart every time he goes in the potty, have I reinforced the behavior? We don't know. It's a trick question. You can't tell because I haven't told you the effect on his behavior.

Negative Reinforcement. The second type of reinforcement procedure that is important to understand when addressing challenging behavior is "negative reinforcement." There are a lot of misconceptions surrounding this term. Many people think that negative reinforcement is equivalent to punishment. Others believe that negative reinforcement involves "negative attention" like scolding a child for misbehavior. In fact, the term "negative" does not imply an unpleasant consequence. Instead, it simply means that behavior is strengthened by *removing* something from someone's environment.

Everyday examples of behaviors strengthened by negative reinforcement include: hitting the snooze button on your alarm clock (removing the aversive sound of the alarm from your environment), putting sunglasses on (removing the aversive glare from your environment), or taking off shoes that are too tight (removing the painful sensation from your internal environment). A student who has learned to hit his teacher to escape his work illustrates a negative reinforcement procedure. When he hits his teacher, work gets removed from his environment, and he becomes more likely to hit again under similar circumstances in the future.

Let's try another quick quiz:

1. If I cross one homework assignment off a student's list for each minute that he participates in a group project, and he gradually participates in group for longer and longer periods of time, what type of procedure was this? Negative reinforcement (consequence = homework removed from the environment; effect on behavior = increase).

2. If peers laugh each time that Johnny makes a wisecrack at the teacher, and he makes more and more wisecracks, what type of procedure was this? Positive reinforcement (consequence = peer attention added to Johnny's environment; effect on behavior = increase).

3. If Johnny loses five minutes of recess each time he makes a wisecrack at the teacher, and he makes more and more wisecracks, what type of procedure was this? Negative reinforcement (consequence = recess (which to Johnny might mean difficult social demands and unstructured time) removed from his environment; effect on behavior = increase).

4. If Teresa earns a quarter toward the price of a movie ticket each time she washes the dishes at her group home, and she volunteers for dish-washing duty more and more often, what type of procedure is this? Positive reinforcement (consequence = quarters added to Teresa's environment; effect on behavior = increase).

5. If I move farther away from a student who is uncomfortable with my proximity each time that he screams, what type of procedure was this? This is another trick question; the effect on behavior wasn't mentioned.

Punishment

A second type of consequence that might follow a behavior is punishment. The specific consequence is technically referred to as a "punisher." A *punisher* is any consequence that decreases the strength (future probability, intensity, or duration) of a behavior. An example of a punisher is your spouse telling you, in a lukewarm tone, that you look "fine" in your carefully selected outfit. The future probability of your wearing that outfit will surely decrease. A school-based example of a punisher might involve assigning extra homework to a student as a consequence for disruptive behavior during the school day. If it decreases the future probability of the disruptive behavior, then this consequence is acting as a punisher.

Just as with reinforcement, there are positive and negative punishment procedures. In a positive punishment procedure, something is added to the environment (e.g., a lukewarm "fine" or extra homework) that weakens a behavior. The particular thing that is added to the environment leading to the decrease in behavior is sometimes referred to as an "aversive." In contrast, with a negative punishment procedure, something is removed from the environment, leading to a decrease in a behavior. For example, you might take car privileges away from your teenaged daughter for a specified period of time if she gets home past her curfew. In this case, the hope is that losing this valued privilege for a while will decrease the probability of her coming home late once her privileges are returned. Similarly, a child might lose ten minutes of television time for each disrespectful comment made to a teacher

Keep It Simple Summary

1. A reinforcer strengthens (increases) behavior.
2. A punisher weakens (decreases) behavior.
3. The term "positive" means that something is added to the environment.
4. The term "negative" means that something is removed from the environment.

Consequence-Based Procedures

	Reinforcer	Punisher
Positive	Adding something strengthens behavior	Adding something weakens behavior
Negative	Taking away something strengthens behavior	Taking away something weakens behavior

at school. The goal of this would be to decrease the future probability of disrespectful comments made to teachers.

Generally speaking, items that might be effective as positive reinforcers are candidates to be removed as part of a negative punishment procedure (e.g., tokens toward a reward, privileges, etc.), as their loss will likely lead to a behavior change.

Like reinforcement, the term "punishment" is defined by its impact on behavior. Therefore, giving a student M&Ms can actually be a punisher if it decreases a behavior, and yelling at him can actually be a reinforcer if it increases his behavior. It is only the effect on behavior that determines which procedure has taken place.

2) Motivation

Motivation, in everyday language, refers to what a person wants or desires, as well as how hard he is willing to work to get it. For example, someone might be motivated to get out of work early for a long weekend or motivated to attain good grades in school.

In the study of behavior, the meaning of the word *motivation* is very close to this but with one major difference. In behavior analysis, we think of motivation in terms of external, measurable factors. When we think of motivation as something internal, as in the colloquial use of the word, that doesn't leave us any way to observe or control it. For example, if we say someone wants to get out of work early for a long weekend, we cannot measure how much he wants this. If we say that someone is motivated to attain good grades in school, we cannot directly increase or decrease this desire. Because motivation drives behavior, if we cannot measure or control it, we cannot change behavior. In the section below, we will describe a strategy developed by behavior analysts to quantify and alter motives.

Motivating Operations (MOs)

Led by the work of Sean Laraway, Jack Michael, and their colleagues (2003), behavior analysts have developed a more quantifiable way to think about motivation referred to as **motivating operations** or **MOs**. You can think of these as "operations" on someone's environment that "establish" a motivation for certain items or events (an **establishing operation** or **EO**), or that weaken motivation for certain items or events (an **abolishing operation** or **AO**). To work with MOs, you observe or manipulate what an individual has had access to and draw conclusions about what might be motivating to him at any given moment. For example, while we can't watch a person and learn how hungry he is, we can observe the number of hours since he has last eaten and draw conclusions about how motivated he may be to get some food. Similarly, we cannot measure how much a person wants to get out of work early to start his vacation, but we can measure the number of months since his last vacation.

Thinking about MOs also highlights the ever-changing nature of motivators. Consider this scenario: For a teen who hasn't eaten all day, pizza will certainly be an effective positive reinforcer for completing chores. In everyday language, we can say that the teen is motivated to eat. As behavior analysts, we can say that an establishing operation for food is in effect. However, with every bite of pizza, the teen becomes less food-deprived, and therefore less motivated to eat more. Let's say our teen has now polished off a whole pizza. Offering pizza as a consequence for completing chores now will be unlikely to strengthen the behavior, and may even act as a punisher for completing chores. Eating the pizza acted as an abolishing operation, making additional pizza less and less desirable. MOs help us understand the frustrating reality that the strongest motivator for your child one day will not necessarily be effective at all the next day.

Some readers may have seen this effect in their own experience. For example, a commonly used intervention for children with autism who have a behavior problem is a technique referred to as a *DRO (differential reinforcement of other behavior)*. This technique involves offering the person a reward for every interval of time that passes when a specified problem behavior has not occurred. Sometimes an interval as brief as one minute may be used. Often, parents or teachers use the child's favorite treat for this procedure.

Not infrequently, a DRO may be wildly effective at first and then stop working. This often baffles the parents or teachers running the intervention. When we consider the impact of the MO on this situation, the reason becomes clear. Let's say someone who bites his own hand is on a one-minute DRO schedule earning M&Ms. That means that every minute that passes without hand biting, he is given one M&M. After one hour, he has eaten 60 M&Ms. After two hours, he has eaten 120 M&Ms. After four hours, he has eaten 240 M&Ms. As much as anyone enjoys M&Ms, how many minutes will pass before he or she throws the bag of M&Ms on the floor? Like the pizza, the M&Ms that were initially reinforcing can also become a punisher.

Motivating operations will be in constant flux. You can think of MOs as being on a continuum (see below) from deprivation (too little) to satiation (too much). As time passes without the individual having access to something, the MO moves left on the continuum toward *deprivation*. As the individual enjoys more and more of something, the MO moves right on the continuum toward *satiation*. MOs apply to everything in the environment, from basic needs such as food, drink, or temperature, to objects and activities such as a favorite toy or game. Different types of stimulation, such as music or touch, as well as social interaction of different types, such as speaking softly, intense reactions, or physical contact, are all subject to MOs.

Similarly, MOs apply to aversive stimuli, which may include loud noises, pain, noxious tastes or odors, etc. In this case, the individual will be motivated to move toward deprivation.

MO CONTINUUM

Deprivation ◀━━━━━━━━━━▶ **Satiation**

In addition to satiation and deprivation, there are other conditions that affect MOs. Think about the last time you went to a bar. There were likely salty or spicy snacks offered for free, such as pretzels, wasabi nuts, or snack mix. As a bar's patrons eat these snacks, they get thirstier and thirstier, leading them to buy more drinks. Similarly, some restaurants use scents or free samples to create a motivation for you to purchase an item you might not have otherwise. Only the most disciplined mall shoppers can resist buying a pretzel or cinnamon bun after getting a whiff while walking by, and only the most self-controlled boardwalk visitors avoid entering the fudge shop after trying the free samples being shared outside.

Establishing operations (EOs), the type of MO that makes an item or activity more likely to act as a reinforcer, have two effects on behavior. The first is giving certain consequences the power to strengthen behavior. In other words, EOs establish reinforcers. For example, when Anthony's parents deprive him of access to his favorite beads, the beads become a potent reinforcer for any behavior that leads to playing with them (such as hitting his head against the window). The second effect of an EO is that it will often evoke behaviors that have led to reinforcement in the past. So, being deprived of his favorite beads for a certain period of time will often trigger head banging against the window for Anthony.

Remember, an EO is not always for something tangible. For example, being deprived of music or social praise makes those consequences more reinforcing as well (Vollmer & Iwata, 1991). Sometimes we notice that children are more likely to engage in a problem behavior because they are "bored." A technical way to think of being bored might be deprivation of stimulation or preferred activities.

The amount of deprivation that will evoke a given behavior varies from person to person. You can think of this as a given individual's threshold. Whenever that threshold is reached, the target behavior will result. This threshold is ever-changing and is affected by remote events such as not getting enough sleep, fighting with your spouse in the morning, or feeling a little under the weather. For example, I may not typically be motivated to respond to someone cutting me off on the highway by yelling expletives to myself in the car (automatic reinforcement), but if I wake up late in the morning, rush to get ready only to be held up by the babysitter arriving late, stop for coffee anyway and discover the line is too long, and then get cut off on the highway, my threshold for motivation to perform that behavior is lower and it will take less external input before I start swearing.

Keep It Simple Summary

MOs are a way to think about motivation. The more you are deprived of something desired, the more you will want it. You will try behaviors that have worked in the past to get it, and getting what you want will strengthen the behavior that worked.

3) Antecedents

The next variable in the learning equation is the immediate antecedent. Broadly speaking, an **antecedent** is whatever changes in the environment the moment before a behavior occurs. For example, in our introduction, we met Jamaal, who makes odd faces and adopts unusual postures whenever other children try to interact with him. In this example, what the peer says or does is the immediate antecedent to the behavior.

There are different types of antecedents that are important in functional behavior assessment. The first type of antecedent acts as a cue that reinforcement is available for performing a certain behavior. For example, an "open" sign on the door of Dunkin' Donuts acts as a cue that coffee is available if you order and pay for it. For someone deprived of coffee (an EO is in effect), the open sign on the door provides a cue that reinforcement is available for coffee-purchasing behaviors. Similarly, for a child deprived of social praise (an EO for praise is in effect), the appearance of someone who has provided social praise in the past provides a cue that reinforcement is available for behaving in ways that have evoked praise before. This person's appearance on the scene acts as a big "open" sign just as one on a Dunkin' Donuts' door might. The technical name for these types of antecedents, which prompt someone to engage in a behavior in order to receive reinforcement, is a *discriminative stimulus* or S^D.

Another type of antecedent that is important in understanding challenging behavior is one that has been associated with punishment for a certain behavior in the past. For example, Dad walking into the room might be this kind of antecedent for a teenager who is smoking. Dad's appearance may cue him to hide his cigarettes if he has learned that smoking in his father's presence will result in punishment (even though more desirable consequences may be available for this behavior in the presence of his friends). This special type of antecedent is called a *punishing stimulus* or S^P. The presence of S^D's and S^P's in an individual's world help determine whether or not he will perform a certain behavior at a given time.

Finally, there are *novel or neutral antecedents.* These are events that may have never occurred in the past or may not have been paired with consequences significant to you in the past. Some of these events will evoke behavior because you associate them with other similar events. For example, if an insect that you have never seen before lands on your arm, you might swat it because of its association with mosquitoes or bees landing on your arm—an event that may have been paired with aversive consequences in the past. Other unfamiliar events may evoke novel responses from you as you attempt to respond effectively to them. For example, if you buy a new water toy for your child, you may try an extensive repertoire of actions, attempting to fill it up, before you stumble on the behavior that leads you to reinforcement (succeeding in filling the toy as you were motivated to do). In the future, that toy will serve as an S^D for the filling response that worked. In sum, learning is constant and ongoing, and these novel or neutral antecedents are an essential part of this process.

Keep It Simple Summary

Antecedents are events that occur just before a behavior. There are three types:

1. an antecedent that cues an individual that a certain behavior will be reinforced (S^D);
2. an antecedent that cues an individual that a certain behavior will be punished (S^P);
3. a novel or neutral antecedent that leads to ongoing learning.

4) Behavior

The final variable critical to learning is behavior. A *behavior* is whatever an individual is doing. Examples include: smoking, making faces and postures, or head banging. Those are problematic behaviors that we want to decrease. However, there are also an infinite number of adaptive or helpful behaviors, such as talking to friends, looking at a speaker, completing homework, washing hands, walking, etc. These are behaviors that we want to increase.

While there are some behaviors that are not observable, such as statements that you make silently to yourself (e.g., "Uh-oh, I can't remember that woman's name—is it Joan? Jada? Jill? Oh no, she's coming over here!"), this book will focus on public and observable behaviors only. For more information on unobservable, private events, see B. F. Skinner's (1953) book, *Science and Human Behavior,* or his (1984) article on the subject, "The Operational Analysis of Psychological Terms."

When designing an intervention for a problem behavior based on learning, we will consider all types of behaviors, rather than just challenging behaviors. Just as hitting your brother is termed a "behavior," handing your brother a cupcake is also called a "behavior." For every behavior that we will attempt to decrease using functional assessment, we will also identify at least one other behavior that we'd like to see more of. To complete a functional assessment, we will need information on an individual's skills as well as his deficits. As we will see in the next section of the book, when intervening with challenging behaviors, we have to be very precise in our thinking about behaviors. As part of a functional assessment, we will develop careful definitions of specific behaviors and ensure that we define our target behaviors using measurable and reliable terms.

> **Keep It Simple Summary**
>
> A behavior is anything that a person does.

Putting the Four Learning Variables Together

In order for learning to occur, all four variables must be in place. For example, consider a child, Jessica, who is learning to ask for juice. If the EO for juice is absent (let's say she just drank two big glasses of juice), then she will not make a juice request, and juice would not act as a reinforcer. Likewise, if Jessica has learned that Mommy cues the availability of juice and Mommy is not in the room, no juice request will occur. If Jessica has an EO for juice, and Mommy comes in the room, but Jessica is involved with a toy and, by the time she looks for Mommy to request the juice, Mommy is already gone, then the behavior of requesting juice will not be strengthened. Finally, if Jessica has an EO for juice, and she sees Mommy, and she requests juice, and Mommy tells her she cannot have juice right now, then requesting juice will be less likely in the future.

Considering all four variables allows us to create the following equations:

$$\text{Motivation} + \text{Antecedent} + \text{Behavior} + \text{Consequence} = \text{Learning}$$

$$\text{EO} + \text{S}^\text{D} + \text{Behavior} + \text{Reinforcement} = \text{Learning}$$

$$\text{Deprivation of juice for a given length of time} +$$
$$\text{the presence of Mommy} + \text{requesting juice} + \text{delivery of juice} =$$
$$\text{Increased likelihood of requesting juice in the future}$$

Keeping in mind that the above assumes that juice is not available without the request, learning has taken place. In the future, under similar conditions (the EO is in effect and the S^D is present), the behaviors are likely to recur.

Learning Theory and Problem Behaviors: The Functions of Behavior

Learning theory explains how people develop particular behaviors. Just as people learn useful behaviors, such as buying coffee or brushing their teeth, they also learn maladaptive behaviors, such as aggression or stereotypic behavior. When we do a functional assessment, we are actually trying to analyze how a behavior was learned. In this way, we can discover how to help someone "unlearn" it, and instead learn a new way to get his needs met. Earlier, a "function" of a behavior was described as the purpose it serves for the individual. Within the context of learning theory, we can offer a more specific discussion of what the term "function" involves.

Understanding a function of a behavior primarily involves a relationship between the EO and the reinforcer. An individual is deprived of something (creating an EO) and is therefore motivated to obtain it (the reinforcer). By analyzing this motivation and reinforcement pairing, we can determine the function of a behavior. In the example described earlier in which Anthony hits his head and obtains beads, the function of the behavior is to obtain the beads. In the example described above in which Grace assaults her peers, the function of the behavior is to obtain peer attention.

The function of the behavior is the "payoff"—the reason for the behavior. The function of the behavior is the message that it communicates: "I want beads" or "I want your attention," for example. Surprisingly, there are a very limited number of messages that a problem behavior communicates. While different professionals characterize these possible functions in slightly different ways, these different systems are equivalent to one another (e.g., Iwata, et al., 1982; Durand & Crimmins, 1988). This book will characterize the possible functions of behavior into four groups:

1. Attention,
2. Objects and activities,
3. Escape/avoid,
4. Automatic reinforcement.

Each of the possible functions is discussed in detail below.

1) Attention

The first possible function of a behavior is to obtain attention. The attention can be of varying qualities. It can involve physical attention such as touching, hugging, or handholding. It can involve vocal attention such as loud, intense reactions, or quieter, milder reactions. It can involve visual attention such as certain facial expressions or more or less animated reactions. Sometimes the function of a behavior is to prevent having to share attention or to obtain attention from a group of individuals. Alternatively, a behavior can function to obtain the attention of one specific individual.

When completing a functional behavior assessment, it is important to consider the specificity of the types of attention that an individual can be motivated to obtain. Otherwise, assessment results can be deceptive. For example, consider a child being cared for by a babysitter while his mother works in her home office. Behavior problems may occur even when he is receiving a rich level of attention from the babysitter. An onlooker might ask, "How can there be an EO for attention when he is receiving so much attention?" Nevertheless, if the child has reached his threshold of deprivation of his mother's attention specifically, and has learned that certain behaviors will cause her to stop her work and intervene, then the function of his behavior might be to get his mother's attention. Similarly, the function of challenging behaviors may be to obtain high intensity attention. An adult may be providing attention that is not very animated or excited, but a certain challenging behavior may bring about a very intense quality of attention.

Sometimes challenging behaviors appear to be spiteful or intentionally aimed at upsetting someone. For example, we have heard about smaller behaviors that were viewed in this way, such as when a teacher complains about a student who taps his desk all day, making a thoroughly irritating noise. We have also seen more complex behaviors viewed in this way, such as when a child destroys a sibling's art project after that sibling refuses to play with him. Even though the sibling may not be present at the moment the art project is destroyed, a certain quality of attention is inevitable later. Similarly, adults may perceive some behaviors as "power struggles." These behaviors may be maintained by a certain intense quality of attention.

As can be seen from the above examples, sometimes children are motivated to obtain attention that doesn't seem desirable to most people. While getting yelled at or moving a sibling to tears might not sound appealing to most, to some children, especially those with social disabilities, these consequences might be pretty attractive. Consider that these types of consequences are relatively predictable, intense, and require little effort to evoke, and the appeal becomes clearer. Furthermore, some children may not have the social skills to distinguish between desirable and undesirable social responses. Therefore, intense laughing and intense yelling may not appear that different to them.

The following is a list of ten common messages that an attention-maintained behavior may be communicating:

1. I want adult attention.
2. I want a particular adult's attention.
3. I want peer attention.
4. I want a particular peer's attention.
5. I want some physical contact.
6. I want a particular form of physical contact.
7. I want an intense emotional response.
8. I want a specific emotional response.
9. I want you all to myself.
10. I want a particular social interaction (e.g., a walk through the hall to "calm down," a deep massage from the OT, etc.).

2) Objects and Activities

Some children engage in problem behaviors as a means of gaining access to preferred objects or activities. This may seem confusing at first. For a child to learn a behavior with this function, he would have to be rewarded with something preferred after he engages in the problem behavior. You might question who would ever do this. When does a child misbehave and then get handed his favorite toy? While this may sound like an unlikely scenario, it actually happens quite often. For example, think about the typically developing child who has learned that if he throws a tantrum in the checkout aisle of the grocery store, his mother or father will buy him a candy bar to get him to stop making such a scene.

Where children with autism are concerned, parents and teachers often use access to object or activities as part of their intervention strategies for managing behavior. Consider Anthony and his beads. It is not at all uncommon for parents and teachers to use distraction or redirection to stop a difficult behavior. Another familiar strategy is to provide calming props, such as stress balls, silly putty, Koosh balls, etc., only when the child engages in challenging behaviors. This may result in a pattern similar to what we saw with Anthony: "I have no putty—I engage in a problem behavior—I have putty." Using various occupational therapy techniques after a challenging behavior (e.g., brushing, deep pressure, or swinging) may also trigger this pattern.

3) Escape/Avoid

As noted above, the most common function of challenging behaviors seen in school settings is escape. Certainly, school is rife with academic demands that a student may be motivated to escape from or avoid. However, children may also use problem behaviors to escape or avoid social demands. For some children, particularly those with autism spectrum disorders, social demands may be perceived as even more challenging than academic demands.

Behavioral researchers William Frea and Carolyn Hughes (1997) completed a functional assessment of inappropriate social behaviors, such as lack of eye contact or exaggerated emotional responses, made by adolescents with developmental disabilities. They found that escape from social interactions served as one function for these behaviors, which had previously been perceived as skill deficits. Jamaal's postures and facial expressions, described in the Introduction, may illustrate this function. Recall that he demonstrated appropriate interaction skills with adults, he engaged in these odd-looking behaviors only when approached by peers, and the behaviors resulted in the peers leaving him alone.

Finally, someone might also exhibit a specific behavior to escape or avoid a certain type of stimulation. Consider the unusual sensitivities experienced by many children with autism spectrum disorders. Lights, sounds, and textures that are innocuous to parents and teachers may be extremely distressing to these children. One preschooler I (BG) worked with had severe tantrums every time she had to get on her bus home. Finally, after some frustrating guesswork, the team decided just to ask her what she didn't like about the bus. She explained that the checkered pattern on the seats hurt her ears. It would have been impossible for any of the team members to predict that looking at a certain pattern would hurt a student's ears. We switched her bus to one with a different pattern on the seats, and the tantrums disappeared.

The following is a list of ten common messages that an escape-maintained behavior may be communicating:

1. I don't want to do this work—it's too hard, too easy, uninteresting to me, or nonfunctional.
2. I don't want to talk to you, or you to talk to me.
3. I don't want you to touch me.
4. I don't want to play this.
5. I don't know how or don't want to manage this unstructured time. This is a very challenging demand for me.
6. I don't want to be around this visual input.
7. I don't want to be around these sounds.
8. I don't want to be around this smell.
9. I don't want to touch this texture.
10. I don't want to eat this food.

4) Automatic Reinforcement

Some behaviors occur in response to internal antecedents and consequences. These behaviors satisfy a need for some type of internal stimulation rather than a need for the more common external motivators. Because the antecedents and consequences for these behaviors cannot be observed, this function (automatic reinforcement) is proposed when no environmental changes are noted before or after the behavior occurs.

While any behavior can serve any function, and one cannot tell the function of the behavior by looking at it, some examples of behaviors that might be automatically reinforcing include: talking to oneself (the sound of one's voice is reinforcing), watching one's fingers (the visual stimulation is reinforcing), or rocking (the kinesthetic feedback is reinforcing).

Hallmarks of this type of behavior are that it can occur when someone is alone or in a very non-stimulating environment, but not necessarily. It can occur any place or time where the self-stimulatory behavior is more reinforcing than whatever is going on outside of the individual's skin. Automatically reinforced behaviors are also common when an individual is experiencing some pain (e.g., biting objects when experiencing a toothache, or banging the side of one's head or pulling one's ears when experiencing an earache). For this reason, if an automatically reinforcing behavior involving the body suddenly crops up in someone who might not have the skills to report pain or discomfort, it might pay to have a quick evaluation from a relevant medical professional.

Behaviors that are automatically reinforcing can sometimes be confused with, or overlap with, behaviors that are associated with brain-based disorders. For example, compulsive behaviors, such as those associated with obsessive compulsive disorder (OCD), occur in response to internal cues and are subsequently reinforced by some type of internal stimulation. These, too, would be identified as automatically reinforcing. Similarly, it can be challenging to distinguish tics from a learned automatic reinforcement behavior, or a learned behavior with some other function. If you do come across a behavior that is difficult to differentiate from another behavioral diagnosis and it turns out to serve an automatic reinforcement function, you may want to consult with a professional who has expertise in the disorder the behavior resembles. Traditional medical or behavioral treatments for other disorders may be effective in individuals with an additional autism spectrum disorder.

While stereotypy (repetitive, non-purposeful behavior) is often assumed to always be automatically reinforced, this is not an accurate assumption. Stereotypy can serve any function. One school-aged child I (BG) worked with who had autism and was also blind provides a clear illustration of how tricky identifying the function of stereotypy can be. During the winter, when the ground was icy, Samantha would jump up and down and flap her hands each day when she got off her school bus. This terrified her mother, who feared that her daughter would injure herself on the ice. Although I began the functional assessment with as open a mind as possible, I had to fight my assumption that jumping and flapping was automatically reinforced. My first clue that something else was going on occurred when Samantha's father mentioned that when he took her off the bus, rather than her mother, the behaviors did not occur.

Further assessment revealed that Samantha's mother responded to the jumping and flapping by putting her arm around Samantha and walking her into the house, which her father did not do. As Samantha had to use her cane to find her way into the house without this assistance and this was a new and challenging skill for her, her mother's guidance made the walk into the house significantly easier for her. To assess the hypothesis that she jumped and flapped to obtain this assistance from her mother, we tried having her mother watch her from the window instead of meeting her at the bus. Samantha immediately stopped jumping and flapping. The S^D signaling reinforcement for this behavior (i.e., her mother waiting at the bus stop) was no longer present. As her mother switched to this routine permanently, the behavior disappeared.

5) Behaviors That Serve More Than One Function

Some behaviors serve more than one function at a time. For example, when a student makes a wisecrack in class, he might be sent to the principal's office (escaping a task) and might also make the rest of the students laugh (accessing peer attention). In this example, one behavior serves two functions at the same time. The same student might make a wisecrack when there is no work demand in order to get peer attention or when he is alone with his teacher in order to escape work. In this case, the behavior serves one function at one time and another function later.

Furthermore, a behavior can serve three functions or all four functions. For example, imagine an adolescent who smears his feces. This behavior may begin as a function of automatic reinforcement: perhaps he was uncomfortable with the feces in his pants and attempts to remove it with his hands. He then wipes his hands off on a nearby object. However, he soon discovers that this makes the staff members at his job site, a 7-11 convenience store, move away from him immediately. He has now learned that smearing feces is an effective means of escaping interactions with these unfamiliar adults. Furthermore, the staff at 7-11 inevitably report this behavior to the job coach. A lengthy interaction with the familiar and preferred job coach may ensue as he scrubs the feces with a particular scrub brush that he enjoys using. The behavior has now been further strengthened by both attention and access to preferred objects. A behavior as powerful as this might even generalize to the next setting, as, if the behavior persists, he is likely to be fired from his current position.

If an individual is using challenging behaviors to communicate multiple functions, this is a cue to the parent or teacher that there is some communication problem. Either the individual needs to develop a more efficient means of communicating basic needs, or, for whatever reason, appropriate communication is not being sufficiently reinforced.

It is also important to note that more than one behavior can be used to serve the same function. A child may have a broad repertoire of behaviors to choose from in getting a certain need met. For example, to escape work, a student might sometimes make wisecracks, sometimes rip up his assignments, and sometimes destroy school property. In this case, the student has many means of communicating the same message. In the next section, we will explore how someone determines which behavior he will demonstrate at which time.

A Special Note on Choice and Control

Clients I have worked with often wonder about the value of control. Do our children sometimes try out a challenging behavior just to have a little power or to assert their right to make choices? I have found that interventions based on the four functions described above are successful without the addition of this "fifth function." Nevertheless, we have probably all seen behaviors that are hard to think of another way.

As a matter of good behavioral "hygiene," to prevent behavior problems, always ensure that your child has plenty of opportunities to direct his own destiny throughout the day. You may be surprised at how many opportunities to make choices you can offer. For example, your child may not be able to choose whether or not to get dressed for the day, but he may be able to choose whether to brush his teeth or put on his clothes first, which shoes to wear, and where to put them on.

How Does My Child Choose a Behavior to Use?

As noted above, a child may have many inappropriate behaviors that all serve the same function. Furthermore, he may have many appropriate behaviors that serve the same function as the inappropriate behavior. For example, let's say that a child's mother is on the phone and he wants her attention. He might say, "Excuse me," he might just start telling her something that happened, he might tell her he needs her to take him to the bathroom, he might pull his baby sister's hair, or he might pour soda on the living room floor. Each of these behaviors has some probability of getting his mother's attention. For most behaviors in a person's repertoire, both appropriate and inappropriate, there are usually many options of behaviors an individual might choose to meet his needs.

Given that many behaviors can serve the same function, how does an individual select which behavior to perform? One answer lies in the efficiency of the behavior. First of all, efficiency is evaluated in terms of how much effort is required to perform the behavior. For example, the young girl with autism who was also blind (described above) figured out that it was easier for her to flap her hands, jump, and be guided up the walk by her mother than it was for her to use her cane.

To encourage an individual to select an appropriate behavior, we have to ensure that he is proficient enough at performing this behavior and that it is not hard work for him. Some people's inappropriate behaviors can be treated by having them practice a simple and appropriate alternative until they can perform it effortlessly. The young man described earlier who was given a picture card to request his cushiony restraint provides an example of this approach.

Next, an individual is more likely to select a behavior that is likely to produce the greatest amount of reinforcement. For example, if raising your hand in class leads to a neutral, "Yes, Johnny," but throwing pencils leads to a very intense, one-to-one discussion in the hallway, a student with an EO for intense attention is likely to request it by throwing pencils. Similarly, whichever behavior gets reinforced the fastest gets priority. If Johnny raises his hand and has to wait three minutes to be called on, or he calls out and gets attention right away, the behavioral pendulum will swing in favor of calling out.

Finally, all of these variables are considered together. The behavior that is ultimately selected represents a balance of:

1. effort required to obtain the reinforcer,
2. quantity of the reinforcer provided, and
3. immediacy of the reinforcer.

Traditionally held beliefs about why behavior occurs all fall someplace within the model described in this chapter. The function of almost every behavior you can think of can be boiled down to either a desire for attention, escape, a particular object or activity, or automatic reinforcement. For instance, on the surface, students who behave well in class may be assumed to be doing so to please the teacher. However, the function of pleasing another person is a subset of obtaining (positive) attention. Or, for another example, in everyday life it is common to attribute someone's behavior to being in a "bad mood." In fact, an individual's mood can change his threshold for motivation to engage in a behavior, but expressing that mood does not actually serve as a function of behavior. (Think of a child with autism who is able to tell his brother "Go away" when he is feeling relatively calm in his own home, but who bites other people to get them to go away when he is in a frightening, unfamiliar environment.) Deciding whether or not to do the "right" thing will also always require a calculation of the balance of effort and reinforcement.

Some behaviors occur due to patterns linked to past learning rather than as a result of immediate reinforcement. For example, reinforcing a two-year-old for sharing, helping others, and being gentle strengthens a broader "response class" (group of related behaviors) that can be referred to as altruism or caring for others. Later, as an adult, this former two-year-old might share food with the poor or rescue someone from a shark as a result of this strong response class, rather than to obtain a specific reinforcer at that moment. In other words, behaviors may be learned according to one of the four functions of behaviors and then be maintained on only a weak or intermittent schedule.

3 | Getting Started: First Steps for Completing a Functional Behavior Assessment

You've mastered the basic concepts of the learning process. Now you're ready to use what you've learned to complete a functional behavior assessment. The next five chapters will cover the assessment process in a step-by-step fashion. These chapters are designed to be a practical guide and are therefore geared toward organization and efficiency. Tips to keep things simple will be offered. The following topics will be covered:

> **Step 1:** Create an assessment team.
> **Step 2:** Select a target behavior.
> **Step 3:** Define the target behavior.
> **Step 4:** Measure the target behavior.
> **Step 5:** Establish a baseline.
> **Step 6:** Interview team members.
> **Step 7:** Observe the behavior.
> **Step 8:** Experiment with the behavior.

Step 1: Create an Assessment Team

Once you have decided to address a particular behavior, the first step is to identify appropriate team members. Careful attention should be paid to this part of the assessment process, as one person's information can be the key to solving the mystery of a problem behavior. Consider the example in Chapter 2 involving Samantha, the girl with autism who was also blind. My consultation visits with the family took place at a day and time when her father was usually at work. Because Samantha's mother was the primary caregiver, I didn't think that this would be a problem. Nevertheless, I happened to come a different day one week and met with Samantha's father. It was his information that ultimately led to identifying the correct function of the behavior.

Ideally, anyone who has seen the targeted behavior should participate on the assessment team, at least in the information-gathering process. Additionally, anyone who is knowledgeable about the child's patterns of skills and deficits, particularly related to communication, should participate as well. Even if an individual has not seen the behavior firsthand, he or she may be able to contribute information about variables in place and the skills being practiced when the behavior does *not* occur.

Family Members

Usually, the team begins with the child's family. Although parents play the most pivotal roles on an assessment team, even a preschool-aged sibling might be able to offer insights about what is likely to set off or prevent a behavior. It is surprising what good behaviorists young children can be! Probably out of necessity, they are often very skilled in recognizing cues that a problem behavior is coming. Some siblings can easily prevent or escape a problem behavior, while others might actually have some experience intentionally provoking the problem behavior. Anyone with an older brother or sister who has been a victim of silent poking, prodding, or pinching, only to get in trouble for the louder and more public retaliation, recognizes this ability in siblings.

Professionals

Professionals who support the family in meeting their child's needs should also participate on the assessment team. This might include the child's teacher, speech therapist, occupational therapist, or home programmer, among others. These individuals may each have different observations and experiences with the problem behavior. Furthermore, each may have different insights into the child's pattern of skills and deficits that has made the problem behavior the most efficient choice for her in getting what she needs.

The assessment process suffers when people who might be aware of variables affecting the problem behavior are excluded. To prevent this from happening on your assessment team, try to think out of the box. Include everyone who might have helpful information. Would your child's bus driver possibly have seen the problem behavior? Are the "specials" teachers (e.g., Art, Music, Physical Education) included in the team meeting? Would your child's grandparents have valuable input? How about the lunch aide? Or the playground monitor?

Be sure to consider all possible contributors. Also, try to allow each observer to speak for him- or herself. If you allow one person to summarize the thoughts of another, you risk losing something critical in the translation.

Peers

Peers are an often overlooked, but potentially valuable, source of information about children in regular education settings. Like siblings, peers may be very skilled at recognizing what sets off a problem behavior and knowing how to prevent it. Nevertheless, asking peers for information requires keen sensitivity to the confidentiality needs of the child with ASD. If a peer witnesses a problem behavior, it is relatively easy for educational staff to say, "What happened over here?" as they would with any other student.

However, in investigating an ongoing problem behavior that hasn't just occurred, questioning a peer requires more judgment. A first consideration is whether or not peers are aware that a given child has special needs. If peers are aware of their classmate's special needs, then approach peers casually without drawing any undue attention to the student. You might say something like this: "I've noticed that you boys usually play on the same equipment as Johnny does on the playground. I've also noticed that he often bites his hand when he is playing there. He really likes that equipment, so I hate to keep him from it, but I don't want him to hurt himself. Do you boys have any ideas about what might set him off there? Or do you have any ideas about how to prevent him from biting his hand?" You might be surprised by the insightfulness of their responses. You can also use this kind of approach to address problems in the peers' own behavior (e.g., "How can we help you stay in your seat until the end of lunch?") so that these types of conversations about a student with special needs won't stand out.

Sometimes peers are not aware that a child has any special needs. In this situation, team members must either seek parents' permission to share this information, or prioritize preserving the child's confidentiality. One strategy some teachers use to gather information without sacrificing confidentiality is to solicit ideas during a group discussion about problem behaviors in the class more generally. In the midst of exploring factors leading to calling out, teasing, etc., the target behavior can be discussed after laying a ground rule with the group that no names will be used.

Another strategy teachers might use is to distribute questionnaires to the class, asking the students to identify a problematic behavior that they observed another child perform, and then answer questions about it. For example, you might ask the class to: "Name a behavior that you have seen at school that causes a problem for the student performing the behavior or for those around him or her. Answer the following questions with that behavior in mind." You can then progress to asking what typically happens before or after the behavior, and other assessment-based questions posed at an age-appropriate level. Responses can then be used as part of a broader discussion of citizenship, but peer observations about the problem behavior are now available. This strategy will only work if the problem behavior is dramatic enough that a significant number of peers are likely to choose that as their target behavior.

The Person with Challenging Behavior

A final critical source of information that is also often overlooked is the person with the problematic behavior. Recall the preschooler who shared that the checkered pattern on the bus seats hurt her ears. Information this specific would never have been available through an observer.

When working with a child or adult who can communicate with you, you can simply ask a few questions about why the behavior occurs or when it is hardest to resist. This sometimes provides tremendous insight and should be a routine part of the assessment process. In fact, students as young as fifth- through eighth-graders have successfully completed extensive assessment interviews geared toward identifying the causes of their own problem behaviors with results that were similar to those of their teachers (Reed, Thomas, Sprague & Horner, 1997). An alternative functional assessment interview has been used with elementary school children, but preliminary investigation seems to suggest that the age of the responder may influence the interview's usefulness (Kern, Dunlap, Clarke & Childs, 1994). Examples of assessment interviews are on pages 63-68.

Assigning Roles to Team Members

Each team member will have a specific role in the functional behavior assessment process. The **team leader or coordinator** has the most central role. This person's job description includes arranging communication among team members, overseeing the implementation of assessment procedures, and making decisions about how data will be collected and analyzed. This person needs strong organizational skills as well as a solid understanding of functional behavior assessment. Typically, this role falls to a parent, a teacher, or a behavior specialist helping with the behavior.

Next, some team members will act as **informants.** They will answer interview questions, take data as assigned to them by the coordinator, and report any observations or ideas. These are great roles for siblings, grandparents, specials teachers, etc. Finally, some team members may **assist the team leader** in analyzing and interpreting the data. This might be a behavior specialist helping a teacher (or vice versa), a teacher helping a parent (or vice versa), etc. Roles should be assigned based on interest, commitment, and expertise, rather than on title.

> ### Keep It Simple Summary
>
> Take information from whomever you can! Be sure that the assessment team has a leader to coordinate and organize team members and information. And don't forget to get information from the individual with ASD whenever possible too!

Step Two: Select a Target Behavior

Many children with autism spectrum disorders have more than one problematic behavior. Deciding how or where to start in improving behavior often poses a challenge. The guidelines that follow will help the team focus and prioritize in order to make their to-do list a manageable one.

Guideline 1: Address Only One Behavior at a Time

If at all possible, focus on just one behavior at a time. As we proceed in describing the assessment process, you will see that treating each behavior requires observation, data collection, and, ultimately, a plan to address it. In other words, tackling each behavior problem involves a significant amount of work. Targeting more than one behavior at a time may overwhelm team members. This may lead them to cut corners in their data collection, observe less closely, or feel hopeless in achieving their goals. As a result, this may slow down the successful assessment for all behaviors. Instead, to the extent possible, limit the demands on team members, consequently setting them up for success in the assessment process.

Additionally, remember that people with autism spectrum disorders often have more than one behavior that serves a particular function. Assessment results for one behavior could lead to an intervention that addresses all behaviors with this function. An intervention plan based on a functional behavior assessment of one behavior often affects other behaviors as well. After addressing the first behavior, the other behaviors may no longer require intervention. For example, let's revisit our wisecracking, homework-ripping, property-destroying student who is motivated to escape his work. A functional assessment of wisecracking alone would lead to an intervention geared toward escape from work—perhaps the work would be peppered with topics he enjoys and he would be allowed to request breaks each day by raising his hand and asking appropriately. This would not only decrease wisecracking, but would also decrease any other behavior serving an escape function.

Guideline 2: Habilitation

A general guideline that behavior analysts use when deciding what to teach is referred to as **habilitation.** This means that you develop goals designed to increase someone's access to naturally occurring, unplanned reinforcement and minimize her access to naturally occurring, unplanned punishment. For example, if Gary, a young child with ASD, desperately wants to make friends, but the other children avoid him because he spends a lot of time talking about fonts, then intervention might start by decreasing font-talk around peers. This would increase Gary's opportunities to get positive feedback from peers.

Similarly, if an adolescent girl gets kicked off of a city bus for sitting too close to people, and she needs the bus to get to the after-school job that she loves, then the first behavior to assess would be sitting too close to people. This would ensure that she keeps her job, through which she receives reinforcement.

According to the principle of habilitation, behavior problems that interfere with adaptive functioning for the individual or members of her community must be addressed right away. Examples might include behaviors that prevent a student from completing her work in school, that prevent peers on a sports team from hearing the coach's instruction, or that prevent a child from taking care of her hygiene at home.

Be careful to avoid addressing behaviors simply because they annoy you. This violates the principle of habilitation. For example, if a student hums quietly while completing written tasks, and only does this with her one-to-one instructor, there is no reason to address this behavior. If she can still learn and will not be handicapped by this behavior in any way, then there is no impact on her access to reinforcement or punishment. If she wants to hum quietly for these tasks, it is her right to choose to do so. Since I've never met a parent or teacher with too much time or energy on their hands, it would be a shame to waste precious resources on a problem that will not change the individual's life in any way. It would certainly be easier for the instructor to learn to tolerate her student's humming.

In contrast, let's imagine that the student above hummed in her inclusive classroom, on the bus, and at the mall. Let's further imagine that her peers made fun of her for this and refused to sit near her in school. This would be an example where the same behavior was leading to naturally occurring punishers, which may unfortunately not be strong enough to stop the behavior on their own. In this case, a functional assessment–based intervention would be warranted.

Guideline 3: Be Safe

Always address behaviors that pose a danger to self, others, or property before addressing less threatening concerns. Preserving the safety of the person with ASD and those around him or her takes precedence over everything else.

Usually, you will complete a functional behavior assessment on a dangerous behavior as you would with any other behavior. However, some behaviors are so dangerous that something must be done immediately as a stopgap and the assessment must wait. In this case, you would be using a crisis management approach.

The basic principle behind crisis management is finding strategies to avoid the behavior or minimize its impact in the moment that it occurs rather than making any long-term improvement in the behavior. Unfortunately, this might even mean that you need to reinforce a problem behavior. Once everyone is safe, a more thorough and long-term approach can be identified. For example, if a student is throwing objects at classmates to escape a task, remove the task immediately to preserve the other children's safety, even though this reinforces the problem behavior. After everyone is safe, then you can begin to think of an assessment plan. Crisis management is discussed again in Chapter 11.

Guideline 4: Set the Child and the Assessment Team Up for Success

After you have followed the above guidelines, if there are still multiple options of behaviors to address, tackle the simplest problem behavior first. This will allow the child and the intervention team to experience success, which is likely to breed more success in the future. Typically, the newest behavior or the behavior that occurs in the fewest settings will be the easiest to assess and ultimately treat. Similarly, if a problem behavior seems fairly straightforward as you think about why it might be occurring, that behavior might be a good choice for a starting point.

Guideline 5: Consider the Needs of Significant Others

In combination with the above guidelines, consider the needs of significant others when selecting a target behavior. For example, a family may have time constraints that make assessment of a particular behavior urgent. Perhaps a child has a behavior problem that occurs in crowds, and her older sister is getting married in three months. This behavior would need to be targeted immediately.

Alternatively, a problem behavior may restrict a family's participation in valued activities (e.g., attending religious services or going to concerts). Then this behavior becomes a priority. Finally, some challenging behaviors make everyday life difficult for family members. One teenaged sibling that I (BG) met with had a brother who stripped in public. She was terrifically embarrassed to ever leave the house with her family and avoided doing so at all costs. Behaviors with such a strong impact on others cry out for immediate attention.

Practice Examples

Let's do a couple of quick practice examples in selecting a behavior to target:

Joe

Joe is a twelve-year-old boy with ASD and intellectual disabilities who is included in a regular education classroom. Joe has been included for three years and has formed wonderful relationships with his peers, which he deeply values. This year, Joe is exhibiting more problem behaviors than he has in the past. Specifically, he makes a clicking sound with his mouth, which most people do not notice, but his teachers, who know him very well, can detect. Additionally, he is laughing loudly and inappropriately during class. When he does this, his teachers give him a stern look, which prompts Joe to engage in a lengthy discussion with them about whether or not they are mad at him. Finally, Joe has started biting others. To date, he has bitten two peers and a teacher. Where should we start with Joe?

The first behavior to address with Joe is the biting. This is a dangerous behavior and therefore takes priority. This is also a good place to start because if he continues to bite peers, his relationships with them may fall into jeopardy (minimizing his access to reinforcement). Additionally, the biting is a relatively new behavior and therefore will be the most likely to respond to assessment and intervention. Next, the team will target his non-contextual laughing. This distracts his peers and may interfere with their learning. It also interferes with Joe's learning, as it results in lengthy discussions with teachers that ultimately take time away from work. Finally, there is no reason to address the clicking sounds. They do not impede his progress in any way.

Tracy

Tracy is an adult with high functioning autism who lives in a supervised apartment. She desperately wants a romantic relationship but has not yet found the right partner. In fact, she has not yet formed any peer friendships, which she also craves. While Tracy speaks easily about topics that interest her with familiar caregivers, she will not respond to her peers' attempts to interact with her. During planned social groups, she is likely to engage in disruptive behaviors such as breaking task materials, as well as aggressive behaviors such as throwing materials at other people in the group.

The first behavior to address for Tracy is the aggression. As with Joe, dangerous behaviors take priority. Additionally, it is likely that only so many instances of aggression will be tolerated before she is asked to leave the social group. Because Tracy is so interested in forming relationships, the group is a critical potential source of reinforcement for her. Next, breaking task materials could be addressed, for similar reasons. Finally, failure to respond to social initiations must be targeted. This behavior clearly thwarts Tracy's goals for herself and should be addressed through the functional assessment process rather than chalking it up to a skills deficit or anxiety.

Keep It Simple Summary

Always address dangerous behaviors first. Next, consider behaviors that are impeding access to reinforcement or leading to undue punishment for the individual, her community members, or her significant others. All other things being equal, address the behavior that is most likely to respond to treatment the quickest. This gives the team and the individual some momentum to build upon.

Step 3: Define the Target Behavior

Many parents and teachers are confused when I ask them to write a definition of the problem behavior. They might look at me in disbelief and ask, "You don't know what a tantrum is?" The problem is that what I call a tantrum might not be the same as what that parent calls a tantrum. The same is true for head banging, echoing, spitting, screaming, or any other problem behavior you can imagine. Because behaviors are assessed by a team of people who each need to know what the others mean by what they say, it is imperative that a clear definition of the behavior be developed.

The best way to write a definition of a behavior is to jot down instructions to someone else about how to act it out. Pretend you are a director giving instruction to an actor as to how to play the part of your child. Write down exactly what to do. This will lead to a clear definition of the behavior. For example, if we were defining the tantrums of BG's two-year-old son, we would write something like this: "Run to nearest couch, chair, or bed while yelling "No!" and throw self onto the furniture belly first." Anyone reading this description could probably act this out and look just like the little boy. To test whether or not your definition will be functional, write it out and give the definition to someone who has never seen your child's problem behavior. Ask him or her to act it out. If it looks right, then you have a clear definition.

Some problem behaviors are not exactly the same every time. For example, "oppositional behavior" might sometimes involve screaming "No!," sometimes involve pretending not to hear what was asked, and sometimes involve saying "Do it yourself!" When different behaviors tend to occur together or tend to follow the same antecedent, you can group them together with an "or" statement and then address them accordingly. For example, the operational definition for the oppositional behavior described above might be something like this: "When given an instruction, [child] either screams 'No!,' screams, 'Do it yourself!,' or continues whatever he was doing."

Ultimately, you will use your definition to measure the behavior. Depending on what the behavior looks like, you will want to know how many times it occurred, how long it lasted, or how intense it was. Therefore, you must write your definition in a way that allows the behavior to be measured. To the extent possible, try to ensure that each definition clarifies the beginning and end of the problem behavior. It must be clear to the reader when to count a behavior as one long instance of the behavior, or when to start counting anew. If intensity is an issue, each intensity level must be clearly defined.

It is best to choose what to count (how many, how intense, or how long) before writing a definition to ensure compatibility between the definition and the measuring device. For example, you wouldn't want to count the duration of the tantrum with the definition of BG's son's tantrum above. When would you start timing—when he runs or when he throws himself on the couch? When would you stop timing—when he flops onto the couch or when he gets up from the couch? What if he is crying when he gets up from the couch? What if he runs directly to another couch? Is that a new episode to time or the same one? In contrast, that definition would be very easy to use when measuring the frequency of the behavior: each time he runs to a couch and flops on it while yelling is one tantrum. A full discussion of guidelines for deciding what to count will be presented in Chapter 4.

Keep It Simple Summary

To create a definition of a problem behavior, write out instructions for someone to act it out. Actually give the instructions to someone who has never seen the behavior. If he or she acts it out correctly, you have a clear definition.

4 | Measuring Behavior

Once you have identified a problem behavior for intervention, defined it so that anyone can recognize it, and selected a team to help you understand the function of the behavior, you are ready for the next steps in FBA: deciding what parameters you will use to measure the behavior and then using those parameters to measure the behavior before you begin to intervene. Steps for completing both of these tasks are described below.

Step 4: Measure the Target Behavior

As part of our functional behavior assessment, we need to quantify the behavior. This allows us to compare the strength of the behavior in different contexts, to identify trends in the behavior, and to ultimately evaluate whether or not the plan that results from our functional assessment is working. Measurements of the behavior provide the facts upon which our functional behavior assessment is based. Without our data, we would just be guessing at the behavior's function. This section will describe practical strategies to get the measuring done. A blank data sheet for each type of measurement system is included so that you may copy it and use it when you are ready to complete your assessment.

In choosing how to measure a behavior, consider two questions:
1. What will be the easiest way to measure this behavior?
2. What measure will be the most likely to capture behavior change?

You want a measure that all team members can use reliably, as well as a measure that will help you see whether or not the intervention that you develop based on your assessment is working. Some behaviors have a more obvious start and finish than others and do not happen in quick succession with other instances of the behavior. For these behaviors, measuring frequency would be effective. Examples include the tantrum described above and Joe's bites described in Chapter 3, or the number of wisecracks made by our student who wants to escape his work. Other behaviors may not be as discrete. These incidents may involve the same behavior repeating itself in rapid succession (e.g., head-banging), multiple behaviors happening in rapid succession (e.g., an aggressive incident involving hitting, kicking, and biting), or one or a number of behaviors that occur over a long period of time (e.g., crying with or without other tantrum-related behaviors). The best method of documenting improvement for these behaviors would probably be to measure the duration of the event.

Finally, progress in some behaviors can best be measured by changes in intensity. For example, a child who bites his own hand may improve by biting less vigorously over time. A simple definition of levels of hand-biting that might work for this child could look like this:

- **Level One**: hand in mouth
- **Level Two**: hand in mouth; teeth leave marks
- **Level Three**: hand in mouth; teeth draw blood

It is easier to learn to define behaviors based on behaviors that you have actually seen. In order to practice using definitions of behaviors within the context of this book, below are two lists. On the left side of the page are behaviors that many people have seen in classic movies. On the right side of the page are their definitions. Try to match the behaviors with their definitions. In the list of answers, measurement strategies suited for each definition will be identified.

Frequency Recording

Measuring frequency means that you are counting how many times something happens in a given period of time. You might record the number of times a behavior occurs per day. For instance, we could measure the number of comments Darra makes about One-D per day. You could also measure the number of occurrences of a behavior in an hour, a ten-minute sample of time, a semester, or any time period at all.

1. *Home Alone* face	a) Toes touching with heels out forming a "V" with feet, pivot on toes to bring heels in to touch one another, and return to starting position repeatedly
2. Dorothy clicking her heels in the *Wizard of Oz*	b) Runs at victim, knocks him down on ground, punches victim's face repeatedly
3. Norman Bates stabbing his victim in the shower in *Psycho*	c) When holding ball for kicker, pulls ball away as kicker's foot is within 3 inches of making contact with ball
4. Ralphie beating up the bully in *A Christmas Story*	d) Hands on cheeks, mouth open wide, screaming
5. Lucy pulling the football away from Charlie Brown to make him fall	e) Grasping knife handle with one arm held straight over head, arm swings down to put knife in victim and repeat

Answers:
1. d) Use a measure of frequency or duration
2. a) Use a measure of duration
3. e) Use a measure of frequency
4. b) Use measure of intensity or duration (more definition needed for intensity)
5. c) Use a measure of frequency

It all depends on the nature of the behavior and the time constraints of the observer.

If you are observing for the same amount of time each observation, then you can simply jot down the total as your "data point" (record of performance for the day). However, if you are observing for a different period of time each day, then you'll need to calculate a rate. Rate is obtained by dividing the number of behaviors by the length of the observation period. For example, if a student rips his assignment page six times in the course of a six-hour school day, then he is ripping pages at a rate of one per hour (6 rips divided by 6 hours = 1 per hour). If a student calls out 10 times during a 20-minute observation, then he is calling out at a rate of 0.5 per minute (10 callouts divided by 20 minutes = 0.5 per minute).

Measuring frequency or rate is ideal for very discrete behaviors with a clear beginning and end. This data is also very easy to collect because everyone has experience counting; you will not be asking any observers to do something new or unusual for them.

Keep It Simple Strategies

In order to make this type of data collection practical, consider the following tricks.

- Buy a golf counter, keep it in your pocket, and click it each time a behavior occurs. Or use your smart phone—there is a free golf counter app. At the end of the observation period, you can look at the number on the counter to see how many times the behavior has occurred. This will keep your hands free during the day, and you won't need to carry a pen and paper or clipboard around with you. If you need to calculate a rate, be sure to jot down your start time and your end time. Some apps for sale, like Behavior Tracker Pro, will collect and graph this data for you.
- Wrap a piece of masking tape around your wrist and keep a marker in your pocket. You can make a mark on the tape each time the behavior occurs and then put the pen back in your pocket. At the end of the observation period, count up the hash marks on the tape to get your total. Again, you will avoid the need for a clipboard and keep your hands free. Remember to make note of your start time and end time if you need to calculate a rate.
- Keep pennies in your right pocket. Whenever the behavior occurs, transfer one penny to your left pocket. At the end of the observation, count up the pennies in your left pocket to get your total. You can do the same thing with objects in the area where you will be with your child. For example, if the behavior happens in the kitchen, pull one packet of sugar out of the sugar bowl each time the behavior occurs. Again, if you will be calculating a rate, you will need to record your start and end times.
- If carrying a clipboard with you will not interfere with your activity, then you can carry the Frequency Recording Data Sheet in Appendix A with you and simply make a hash mark for each occurrence of the behavior.

Time-Based Measures of Behavior

Duration

Measuring the duration of a behavior involves recording how long a behavior lasts. This type of measure is best suited for behaviors with a large number of component parts (e.g., a fist fight) or that last a long time (e.g., crying episodes). Some other examples of problem behaviors that might be conducive to a duration measure include rocking, tantrums, or off-task behavior. These behaviors may not include discrete episodes or may involve too many component parts of different types to measure. Note that when you measure duration, you automatically get a count of frequency. Each duration you record counts as one occurrence of the behavior.

To measure duration, you simply record the beginning and end time of the behavior and then figure out how long it lasted. You can measure duration in seconds, minutes, or hours. You can then calculate either an average or total duration per observation. A total duration is only appropriate for use when each observation lasts the same amount of time. Otherwise, the totals aren't comparable and an average will provide a better gauge.

You can measure duration of an *inappropriate* behavior during your assessment. This would imply that a longer duration involves more problematic behavior. Alternatively, you can measure duration of *appropriate* behavior during your assessment. Then a longer duration would imply less problematic behavior. For example, for a child who exhibits a variety of problematic, off-task behaviors during math lessons, it will be easier to measure the duration of on-task behavior during this time than to define each possible off-task behavior and measure each one. To measure on-task behavior, you would record the start and end time of each bout of on-task behavior and then calculate a total or average duration.

Latency

Another time-based measure is the latency to a behavior. This refers to the amount of time that elapses between the onset of an event and the start of a behavior. Examples of latency measures include the length of time it takes you to get up after an alarm rings, the length of time it takes a child to begin working after instructions have been given, or the length of time a student participates in group before a problematic behavior occurs. Like duration, latency can be measured in seconds, minutes, or hours. To measure latency, you record the time that a stimulus is introduced or an activity begins (e.g., home-based discrete trial session starts), and then record the time that a behavior occurs (e.g., the child throws materials on floor). The amount of time that passes between the two events is the latency.

Keep It Simple Strategies

In order to make this type of data collection practical, consider the following tricks.

- Use a timer that counts up, or use the clock app on a smart phone that has a timer on it. You can keep it in your pocket and just hit the start and stop buttons at the appropriate time. Keep a paper and pen in a nearby location and then jot down the durations. If you are calculating a total duration, you do not need to write anything until the end of the day or session. The timer will continue to add the durations for you.

- If you are in a room with a clock, look up and remember the start time, or take a photo of the clock with your phone. When the behavior ends, jot down both the start and end times, or take another photo of the clock with your phone. If using pencil and paper, you can either carry a clipboard or supplies in an accessible place (e.g., on the kitchen table for behaviors that occur in the kitchen).

- Buy an eyeliner pencil and a cheap watch with a big face. Keep the eyeliner pencil in your pocket. Mark the watch at the place where the minute hand is when the behavior starts and then again when the behavior stops. This will buy you a little time before you need to get to your data sheet. If you use this approach, be sure to jot the duration down as soon as possible after the behavior ends. If the marks from one occurrence are still on the watch when the next occurrence begins, it will be too confusing to determine which marks are from which behavior. Also, this may become confusing for behaviors that last more than an hour, as it will be unclear which is the start mark and which is the end mark. Wipe the watch face with a baby wipe after recording times on your data sheet.

- Use the Duration of Behavior or Latency to Behavior Data Sheets in Appendix B and Appendix C if you can carry a clipboard and pencil while observing the behavior.

As with duration measures, either an appropriate or inappropriate behavior can be measured. For example, a longer latency to a problem behavior indicates improvement (e.g., more and more time passes before disruptive behavior in groups), or a shorter latency to an appropriate behavior can indicate improvement (e.g., less and less time passes before coming to group when called). Note that when you measure latency, you automatically get a count of frequency. Each latency that you record counts as one occurrence of the behavior. Because this is also time based, you will use the same "keep it simple" measurement strategies as for duration.

Intensity

Tracking the intensity of a target behavior involves dividing the behavior into various degrees of intensity and using that to track any changes. The key to measuring intensity is the creation of a sound and reliable rating system. Consider the following example of an intensity scale for an individual who punches the wall:

Level 1—pounds fist on wall

Level 2—pounds fist on wall repeatedly

Level 3—pounds fist on wall; makes hole

Level 4—pounds fist on wall repeatedly; makes multiple holes (indicate number)

Examples of behaviors conducive to an intensity rating include episodes of aggression, tantrums, or property destruction, or behaviors such as screaming in which the volume changes.

When measuring intensity, you need to record the level of each occurrence. Note that when you measure intensity, you automatically get a count of frequency. Each intensity level that you record counts as one occurrence of the behavior. If you observe for different lengths of time each day, you will need to calculate a rate of occurrence of behaviors at each intensity level. To do this, divide the number of behaviors at each intensity level by the length of the observation period.

Keep It Simple Summary

To make this type of data collection practical, consider using the following tricks:

- Wrap a piece of masking tape around your wrist and keep a marker in your pocket. Jot down the intensity rating on the tape each time the behavior occurs, and then put the pen back in your pocket. At the end of the observation period, transfer data to data sheet.
- Either use a clipboard with the data sheet in Appendix D or keep the data sheet and pen close to where the behavior occurs and jot down the intensity level.

Using Samples of Behavior

All of the measurement approaches described above require the observer to pay attention throughout the entire observation period. Additionally, they are designed for behaviors that are somewhat discrete, in that a beginning and an end can be detected. Not all behaviors or situations are conducive to these approaches, however. Some behaviors may be nearly constant or may happen too rapidly for you to count each occurrence. Sometimes staff or family members have too many other demands to focus solely on one child and one behavior.

For these situations, a group of alternative approaches are available that rely on samples of behavior rather than constant observation. A sample is a little piece of something that represents the whole. For example, if you wanted to know the quality of the water in a reservoir, you wouldn't test every drop. Instead you would take out a little bit of the water and test that to give you a picture of what the whole reservoir is like. In calculating ratings of television shows, networks do not monitor every single person who watches television. Instead, they have boxes in a small group of people's homes that tell them what these viewers are watching, and they use this data to estimate what the entire population of television viewers prefers. Again, this is a sample of the behavior. We can use samples during functional behavior assessments too.

If a behavior is amenable to the measurement systems described above, but the team members do not have the freedom to observe and record the behavior accurately all day long, consider observing for a sample time interval. To do this, first you must identify whether you need to observe throughout the day or just during specified periods. If the behavior only occurs in certain settings (e.g., failure to respond to teacher instruction can only happen during periods of the day when teachers present instruction), then you already have natural limitations on when to observe.

If the behavior is equally likely to happen at any time, it is best to spread out the periods of time that you observe. Let's say that you are a teacher, you are busy with other students, and cannot take detailed data on one student's behavior all day long, but the behavior does happen all day long. Choose three ten-minute periods of time throughout the day during which you will commit to keeping an eye on the student and measuring the behavior. You can use the same ten-minute periods of time each day or rotate through the day randomly to get a broader sample. During this period, you can record the behavior as you normally would have using the measure above that is best suited to the behavior along with the appropriate data sheet.

Some behaviors require different measurement strategies. These include behaviors:

- that do not have a clear beginning and end (e.g., near constant self-talk),
- that occur too quickly to count each one (e.g., hand flapping), or
- that happen too constantly throughout the day to count (e.g., constant humming).

Partial Interval Time Sample

One alternative available for behaviors like these is called a "partial interval time sample." When using this strategy, the observation period is broken into smaller intervals and the observer makes an indication at the end of each interval as to whether or not the behavior occurred at all during that interval. For example, if a student engages in near constant self-talk, we might ask the question, "During how many one-minute intervals per day does the student engage in self-talk?" We are not going to count how many times this behavior occurs during each interval. Instead, we will simply record whether or not the behavior happened at all during that time period.

The key to using this approach is to select a time period that is big enough that you are sure to capture the behavior and small enough to be sure that changes in the behavior can be seen. Identifying appropriate intervals takes practice and you may need to try out a couple of different intervals before committing to one for the full assessment. Or you can select a starting interval by spending one day measuring the time between occurrences of the behavior to identify the longest gap. Then set the observation interval a little smaller than that time period. So, if the child never goes more than ten minutes without self-talk, set your observation period at eight minutes.

To implement this strategy, buy a timer or use the one on your phone and set it for the appropriate interval. Then, when the timer goes off, use the Time Sample Data Sheet in Appendix E to record whether or not the problem behavior occurred during that interval.

Momentary Time Sample

A similar approach that is useful either for the highest frequency behaviors or for team members who cannot watch the individual with ASD through the whole observation period is called a "momentary time sample." This approach also involves identifying an appropriate interval but differs in that the observer only records what is going on at the end of that interval. If the behavior occurred fifteen times before the end of the interval, it does not matter. The only thing that is recorded is what is happening at the moment the interval ends.

To use this strategy, choose an appropriate interval as described in the section above. Then set a timer for the appropriate interval and look at the child when the timer goes off. Record whether or not the behavior is occurring at that moment. For this approach, it is best to use a vibrating timer so the child will not know when he is being observed.

For each of these measurement strategies, if each observation period lasts a different length of time, you will need to calculate a percent of intervals during which the behavior occurred. This will ensure that the numbers used to summarize performance are comparable.

Permanent Products

A final measure of behavior that is by far the simplest to use is referred to as permanent products. When relying on a permanent products measure, you assess naturally occurring, lasting records of a behavior. Some examples might include counting the number of worksheets a child completed, counting the number of holes a student punched in the wall, or counting the number of bite marks on someone's arm. The obvious advantage of this approach is that the data can be recorded long after the behavior is complete. This is especially advantageous for dangerous behaviors, as it frees up the caregiver to maintain safety and attend to the behavior at the time that it occurs rather than having to attend to measurement, without sacrificing measurement.

Of course, this approach will only work with behaviors that actually leave a permanent product. For example, you could not measure rocking with a permanent products measure. In contrast, breaking pencils in half would be conducive to this approach.

Refer to Appendix F for a Permanent Products data sheet.

Step 5: Establish a Baseline

The next step in the assessment process is to establish a baseline. A baseline is a quantitative measure of a behavior in its natural state. In other words, a baseline is a picture of what the behavior would look like if we never did anything specific to address it and we just kept doing whatever we'd been doing all along. For example, to establish a baseline of Jamaal's postures and faces, we would simply measure what he's doing without introducing any intervention. To establish a baseline of wisecracks for the student who made wisecracks in class, we would perhaps count the number of wisecracks.

A common misconception about establishing a baseline is that the behavior is measured while the adult ignores the child's behavior. This will not necessarily provide a baseline. If the adult was not previously ignoring the behavior, then we are not measuring the natural state of the behavior. Instead, we are measuring the behavior under the condition of being ignored. This may change the behavior. For example, imagine if Anthony's parents suddenly stopped giving Anthony his beads when he banged his head, thereby ignoring the behavior. Certainly, Anthony's behavior would change. Maybe his behavior would initially get worse because he was confused that his previously reinforced behavior was not getting reinforced. Maybe he would stop banging his head altogether. Maybe he would try something different to get the beads. We would get one picture of Anthony's behavior from this assessment. Then, as soon as baseline ended and his parents stopped ignoring the behavior, the behavior would look totally different.

You may wonder why establishing a baseline is so critical. Baseline answers the following key questions:

1. What is the general level of the behavior? Measuring the behavior as part of a baseline gives the team a sense of how strong the behavior is. Many times, measuring baseline allows a team to see that a behavior is not as intrusive as they once thought. Sometimes a very disturbing behavior can happen just once or twice and because the nature of the behavior is upsetting, it seems that an intervention is urgently necessary. Nevertheless, the baseline data reveal that the behavior is really very rare and not a priority at all. Establishing a baseline can prevent teams from devoting a great deal of time and energy to a low-level behavior.

Conversely, baseline data may be helpful in convincing a skepti-cal team member that an intervention is, in fact, necessary when the data show the consistency or high level of the behavior. The sample graph below illustrates a low-level behavior. If this graph were mea-suring a highly intrusive behavior, such as aggression, even this low level might be too high and call for intervention. However, if the behavior being measured has less significant effects, such as hum-ming or nail-biting, this behavior may not warrant any intervention, as it is very infrequent.

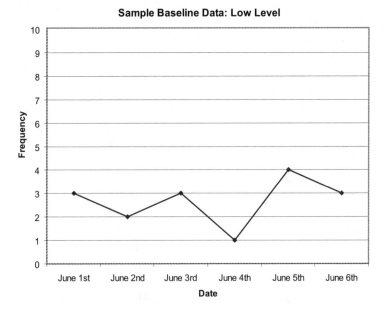

Sample Baseline Data: Low Level

2. Is the behavior getting stronger, weaker, or staying the same? Measuring a baseline allows us to see the direction that a behavior is taking. If a behavior is getting worse or staying at a high level, then further assessment, and, ultimately, an intervention is warranted. However, sometimes baseline data reveal that a behavior problem is resolving on its own. Whatever environmental variables are in place are exactly what is needed for the behavior to go away. In this case, changing the environment by introducing an intervention would present a risk that the behavior would instead get stronger. Because the purpose of an assessment is to inform intervention, there is no need for intervention in that scenario.

Occasionally, a behavior might be weakening, but at too slow a pace. In this case, team members may decide that an intervention is worthwhile, all the while acknowledging the risk of derailing the ongoing improvements. To determine the direction of the behavior, baseline must last long enough to demonstrate patterns of the behavior. One common strategy is to gather three to five "data points"; that is, to measure the behavior on three to five separate occasions. However, this guideline only applies when a pattern is evident within that time period. You may need to extend baseline if a pattern is not evident by that point.

The graph below illustrates a response that is increasing. If this graph represented a maladaptive behavior, then an intervention would certainly be warranted.

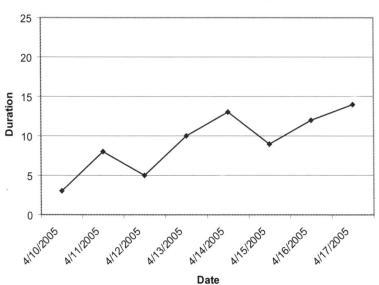

Sample Baseline Data: Increasing Trend

3. Is the behavior consistent or variable? Measuring a baseline allows team members to determine whether or not a behavior is stable. If the behavior is at a pretty consistent level or is following a pretty consistent growth curve, then the team can be assured that the variables that affect the behavior are consistent across settings. If the behavior is variable, meaning that it is sometimes very strong and sometimes very weak, then that gives us a clue that something specific to certain settings or contexts is affecting the behavior. It can be beneficial to give variable behaviors some time to stabilize before intervening, as it might turn out that when a trend is finally apparent, the behavior is decreasing.

The graph below illustrates a behavior with a highly variable pattern. Note that in order to figure out what is going on, labeling the data points is critical. This enables even the most variable data to tell a coherent story.

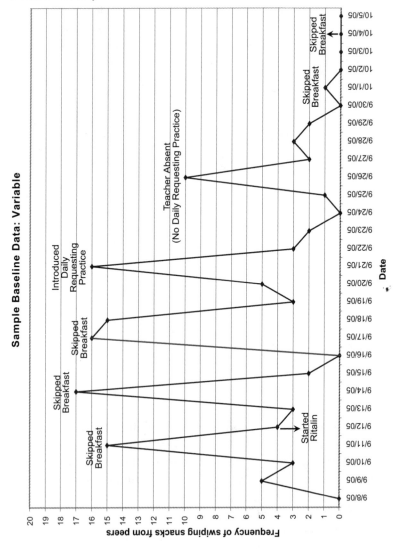

Keep It Simple Strategies

To establish a baseline, measure a behavior while doing whatever you've been doing all along. If it turns out to be a low intensity, low-level behavior, or if the behavior turns out to be decreasing, continue measuring the behavior until it is gone. No other forms of intervention are necessary. If the behavior is very variable, try to identify variables that are in place when the behavior is stronger or weaker. Possible variables include: the people who are interacting with the individual, the time of day, changes in medication, etc.

Finding Out Who Knows What

You have assembled a team of people knowledgeable about the problem behavior you wish to target. At this point in the process, it is time to find out what they know. While you may feel that chatting informally with someone is sufficient, you risk omitting important questions if you don't do a structured interview. Furthermore, you may not allow the interviewee enough time to focus on the behavior problem if you do not create a scenario in which he or she can concentrate on the behavior.

Step 6: Interview Team Members

When you interview someone as part of a functional behavior assessment, your goal is to identify patterns in the behavior that will help you identify the behavior's function or functions. Thinking back to how behaviors are learned will help you figure out what you need to ask your interviewees. Specifically, you will want to ask questions that help you determine the following types of information:

- What the immediate antecedent and consequences of the behavior are.
- What the individual has access to (or escapes from) after performing the behavior that she didn't have access to (or the ability to escape from) before.
- Whether any establishing operations may be in effect. (Does the behavior occur after a long period of deprivation from

something preferred? Or does it occur after a long period of interaction with something nonpreferred?)

- Whether different reporters describe different environmental conditions when the behavior occurs, or whether the same behavior patterns are recurring in different settings.
- How well the individual communicates and the consequences of appropriate communication.

To help get at these questions, a blank, reproducible interview questionnaire is included below. Guidelines for interpreting responses to the questions are also provided.

When interviewing team members, there are a few strategies to keep in mind. First of all, you are looking for facts rather than opinions. The goal of the assessment is to develop and test hypotheses based on facts. This will lead to a more accurate and efficient assessment. Separate opinion from fact whenever possible. For example, if someone says, "I'm sure he's doing this to get attention," that is clearly an opinion. Follow up with a fact-finding question such as, "Tell me some of your observations that have led you to feel this way" or "How can you tell?" If your reporter responds by saying something like "He checks to see if I'm looking whenever he does it," that sounds more like a fact.

Because people's opinions tend to skew their observations and consequently their reporting, it is important to interview multiple reporters. If few reporters are available, feel free to answer the questions in the interview yourself. Try to do this before interviewing anyone else so that your answers are not influenced by others. Also, to protect your interviewees from being swayed by one another, try to interview them individually.

The benefit of using the questions below as an interview rather than as a written questionnaire is that you can follow up on certain answers or clarify certain responses. However, there are times when it will not be feasible to interview each team member who might have valuable information. In those cases, feel free to give them the list of questions to respond to as a questionnaire. Administered as an interview, the following questions will require approximately thirty minutes to complete, depending on the amount of information available.

Functional Behavior Assessment Interview Form

Behavior:_____

Definition of Behavior:

_____

_____

_____

Date: _____

Interviewer (individual asking the questions):_____

Reporter (individual answering the questions): _____

Instructions to Interviewer:

1. Begin by introducing self and role, if necessary.
2. Label target behavior and read definition to interviewee. Before beginning interview, confirm that interviewee has seen the behavior. If yes, proceed with interview. If no, but the person does have other information about the individual who is exhibiting the problem behavior, please ask only those questions relevant to "background information" and "communication skills."
3. Explain to the interviewee that he or she may not have the information to answer each question (e.g., a teacher may not have information about sleep patterns). Ask each question anyway in case they have information that you might not expect.
4. Be sure to solicit examples whenever possible with the goal of distinguishing fact from opinion.

Background Information

1. What is your role in relation to [   ] *(individual's name)*?

_____

2. How long have you known [   ]? _____

3. Does [   ] have a consistent schedule (each day or on some days)? _____

4. If yes, please describe. _____

_____

(Continued on next page.)

5. Does [   ] have a sense of this schedule? Does he or she know what comes next? _____

6. What are [   ]'s favorite things (objects, people, and activities) in this setting? _____

    a. In what situations are these things earned?

    _____

    b. In what situations does [   ] have free access to these things?

    _____

    c. In what situations does [   ] have little or no access to these things?

    _____

    d. For those who have seen the behavior problem: Does the behavior problem vary in each of the above situations?

    _____

7. What are [   ]'s least favorite things (objects, people, and activities)? _____

    a. In what situations does [   ] have inescapable exposure to these things? _____

    _____

    b. In what situations does [   ] have escapable exposure to these things? _____

    _____

    c. In what situations does [   ] have no contact with these things at all? _____

    _____

    d. For those who have seen the behavior problem: Does the behavior problem vary in each of the above situations?

    _____

8. Are there peers/siblings with whom [   ] enjoys interacting? _____

9. Are there adults with whom [   ] enjoys interacting?
_____

10. How much access to social interaction does [   ] have throughout the day? _____

11. Is [   ] well liked by peers/siblings? _____

12. Is [   ] well liked by adults? _____

(Continued on next page.)

13. How does [   ] respond to difficult tasks?

_____

14. How does [   ] respond to interrupting desired activities?

_____

15. How does [   ] respond to withdrawal of attention?

_____

16. How does [   ] respond to sharing attention with
someone else? _____

_____

Communication Skills

1. How does [   ] make his or her wants and needs known?

_____

2. What is the easiest means of communication for [   ]?

_____

3. How does [   ] obtain your attention?

_____

   • What percent of time (approx.) do you provide attention in
     response to this bid? _____

4. How does [   ] let you know when he/she wants to
   socialize with you? _____

   • What percent of time (approx.) does this bid result in
     socialization? _____

5. How does [   ] let you know when he/she wants an
   object or activity? _____

   • What percent of time (approx.) do you provide the object
     or activity in response to this bid? _____

6. How does [   ] request a break from tasks or a
   different task? _____

   • What percent of time (approx.) do you provide a break or
     new task in response to this bid? _____

History of Behavior

1. When did you first notice the target behavior? _____

_____

(Continued on next page.)

2. Were there any changes that you know of that coincided with the onset of the behavior? _____

_____

    a. Were any new demands placed on [   ]?

    _____

    b. Were any demands on [   ] increased?

    _____

    c. Were demands removed or reduced?

    _____

    d. Did the ratio of children to caregivers change at that time?

    _____

    e. Did any children enter or leave the environment at that time?

    _____

    f. Did any adults enter or leave the environment at that time?

    _____

    g. Was the level of attention altered in any way at that time?

    _____

    h. Did [   ]'s schedule or activities change at that time? _____

    i. Did the available materials change at that time? _____

    j. Was there any illness at that time? _____

    k. Was there any medication change at that time? _____

    l. Was there any change in sleep patterns at that time?

    _____

    m. Was there any change in eating patterns at that time?

    _____

    n. Was there any change in [   ]'s physical environment at that time? _____

Present Picture of the Behavior

1. How often do you see the behavior? _____

2. Is it likely to occur with any other behaviors? _____

3. Are there certain situations in which the behavior always occurs?

_____

(Continued on next page.)

4. Are there certain situations in which the behavior never occurs?
   _____

5. Can you evoke the behavior? If yes, how? _____

6. Can you prevent the behavior? If yes, how? _____

7. Is the behavior more intense in some circumstances? If yes, when?
   _____

8. Is the behavior milder in some circumstances? If yes, when?
   _____

9. Are there certain days of the week the behavior is more or less likely to occur? _____
   - If yes, what is different about [   ]'s schedule on those days? _____

10. Are there certain times of day that the behavior is more or less likely to occur? _____
    - If yes, what is going on in [   ]'s schedule at that time? _____

11. Are there certain settings in which the behavior is more or less likely to occur? _____

12. Are there certain people with whom the behavior is more or less likely to occur? _____

13. Are there certain activities during which the behavior is more or less likely to occur? _____

14. Are there certain materials that are usually present when the behavior occurs? _____

15. Are there certain materials that are usually not present when the behavior occurs? _____

16. Have you noticed any common triggers for the behavior?
    _____

17. How do you usually respond to the behavior?
    _____

18. How do others usually respond to the behavior?
    _____

19. Do you think the behavior would happen if [   ] were left alone? _____

20. Have you ever walked in on [   ] performing the behavior when he or she was alone? _____

(Continued on next page.)

Physiological Considerations

1. What medications is [   ] taking right now?

   _____

2. When did [   ] start taking this medication?

   _____

3. What are some common side effects? _____

   _____

4. Why is he or she taking this medication? _____

   _____

5. Does [   ] have any illnesses or conditions?

   _____

   • If yes, do you notice any relationship between [   ]'s
     behavior and the severity of these conditions? _____

6. Describe [   ]'s sleep patterns. _____

   _____

   • Do you notice any relationship between [   ]'s
     sleep and behavior? _____

7. Describe [   ]'s eating patterns. _____

   _____

   • Do you notice any relationship between [   ]'s
     eating and behavior? _____

8. Does [   ] have any known allergies? _____

Functional Behavior Assessment Interview Form
INTERPRETATION GUIDE

Background Information

1. What is your role in relation to [   ] *(individual's name)*?
   Use response to determine areas of interviewee's expertise.

2. How long have you known [   ]?
   Use response to estimate level of interviewee's expertise.

3. Does [   ] have a consistent schedule (each day or on some days)?

   If yes, please describe.
   Use schedule as a reference for baseline data. Compare levels of behavior when the individual has different activities scheduled. Also, compare description of schedule among different respondents. If descriptions conflict, schedule probably varies based on who is with the individual.

4. Does [   ] have a sense of this schedule? Does he or she know what comes next?
   If target behavior consistently occurs prior to a certain activity, possibly delaying it, the individual may be avoiding this activity if he or she is able to predict schedule.

5. What are [   ]'s favorite things *(objects, people, and activities)* in this setting?
   Does interviewee know what child's favorite things are? If no, he or she may not have enough access to preferences. Child also may not be able to communicate preferences. Enriching learner's environment by adding preferred objects and activities, as well as other types of stimulation, may decrease target behavior.

   a. In what situations are these things earned?

   b. In what situations does [   ] have free access to these things?

   c. In what situations does [   ] have little or no access to these things?

   d. For those who have seen the behavior problem: Does the behavior problem vary in each of the above situations?

   These questions are all designed to give clues about the level of enrichment and the relationship between access to

(Continued on next page.)

preferred items and behavior problems. Lower levels of enrichment might be associated with automatic reinforcement behaviors, when a child has nothing else to do, and thereby "entertains" him- or herself with the target behavior. Relatively high levels of behavior problems in situations with restricted access to preferred items or activities suggest that automatic reinforcement might be the function of the behavior.

6. What are [   ]'s least favorite things (objects, people, and activities)?

    a. In what situations does [   ] have inescapable exposure to these things?

    b. In what situations does [   ] have escapable exposure to these things?

    c. In what situations does [   ] have no contact with these things at all?

    d. For those who have seen the behavior problem: Does the behavior problem vary in each of the above situations?

    These questions are all designed to give clues about possible escape behaviors. Also, too much exposure to aversive situations signals the need for an enriched environment. For more on intervention strategies, see Chapter 8.

7. Are there peers/siblings with whom [   ] enjoys interacting?

8. Are there adults with whom [   ] enjoys interacting?

9. How much access to social interaction does [   ] have throughout the day?
These questions are geared to assessing the level of attention that the child has each day, as well as whether or not attention is a motivator for this child.

10. Is [   ] well liked by peers/siblings?

11. Is [   ] well liked by adults?
When learners are not well liked, they typically receive a lower quality or quantity of attention. This might be associated with problem behaviors maintained by attention (i.e., the individual may be engaging in the problem behavior so that others will pay attention to him or her).

12. How does [   ] respond to difficult tasks?
To assess possible escape-maintained behaviors.

(Continued on next page.)

13. How does [   ] respond to interrupting desired activities?
    To assess behaviors maintained by access to objects or activities.

14. How does [   ] respond to withdrawal of attention?
    To assess behaviors maintained by attention.

15. How does [   ] respond to sharing attention with someone else?
    To assess behaviors maintained by attention.

Communication Skills

1. How does [   ] make his or her wants and needs known?

2. What is the easiest means of communication for [   ]?

3. How does [   ] obtain your attention?

    • What percent of time (approx.) do you provide attention in response to this bid?

4. How does [   ] let you know when he/she wants to socialize?

    • What percent of time (approx.) does this bid result in socialization?

5. How does [   ] let you know when he/she wants an object or activity?

    • What percent of time (approx.) do you provide the object or activity in response to this bid?

6. How does [   ] request a break from tasks or a different task?

    • What percent of time (approx.) do you provide a break or new task in response to this bid?

All of the above questions are geared toward assessing the efficiency of using appropriate versus inappropriate behaviors to obtain what is wanted. If a deficit in communication skills is identified, an intervention might focus on building skills in this arena rather than addressing the target behavior directly.

History of Behavior

1. When did you first notice the target behavior?
   This question helps assess how long the behavior has been a problem in this particular setting. By interviewing multiple

(Continued on next page.)

informants, it is possible to determine where the behavior first appeared. This may offer a clue as to the function. If a behavior problem has been around so long that the staff members cannot recall when the behavior began, that just suggests that it might take a little longer for the intervention to work, as the behavior has such a long learning history to "unlearn." Just skip the following section and move on.

2. Were there any changes that you know of that coincided with the onset of the behavior?

    a. Were any new demands placed on [   ]?

    b. Were any demands on [   ] increased?
      To assess a possible escape function of the behavior.

    c. Were demands removed or reduced?
      Unstructured time is often very demanding for people with autism. This question therefore assesses behaviors related to escape from the demand of needing to fill one's own time or sitting quietly, etc. Also, a sudden increase in downtime might be associated with an increase in automatic reinforcement behaviors.

    d. Did the ratio of children to caregivers change at that time?

    e. Did any children enter or leave the environment at that time?

    f. Did any adults enter or leave the environment at that time?

    g. Was the level of attention altered in any way at that time?
      These questions are geared toward assessing attention-related variables. A behavior problem may also involve escape from the attention of a non-preferred person.

    h. Did [   ]'s schedule or activities change at that time?

    i. Did the available materials change at that time?
      These questions are geared toward assessing behaviors related to objects and activities.

    j. Was there any illness at that time?

    k. Was there any medication change at that time?

    l. Was there any change in sleep patterns at that time?

    m. Was there any change in eating patterns at that time?
      These questions are geared toward assessing any physiological factors affecting the behavior. These can either alter someone's threshold for behavior, "shortening

(Continued on next page.)

their fuse," so to speak, or may be associated with automatic reinforcement behaviors. This information will also help clarify whether or not a certain behavior problem may be a side effect of a medication.

n. Was there any change in [   ]'s physical environment at that time?
This question is geared toward assessing whether the individual may be responding to some sort of stimulation from the physical environment, either escaping an unwanted sensation, or reacting to a higher level of distraction, etc.

Present Picture of the Behavior

1. How often do you see the behavior?
The answer to this, along with baseline data, allows comparison across settings.

2. Is it likely to occur with any other behaviors?
The answer to this allows hypothesis for other behaviors that might serve the same function. For example, if head-hitting and hand-biting usually occur together, they are likely to serve the same function

3. Are there certain situations in which the behavior always occurs?

4. Are there certain situations in which the behavior never occurs?
Identify characteristics of each setting as a clue to the function of the behavior. For example, if it always happens during work and never during breaks, it is probably escape related.

5. Can you evoke the behavior? If yes, how?
This answer will specify at least one of the immediate antecedents.

6. Can you prevent the behavior? If yes, how?
Identifying variables that prevent a behavior gives clues to motivation. For example, if behavior can be prevented by seating the child alone, behavior may occur to escape attention.

7. Is the behavior more intense in some circumstances? If yes, when?

8. Is the behavior milder in some circumstances? If yes, when?

9. Are there certain days of the week the behavior is more or less likely to occur?

   • If yes, what is different about [   ]'s schedule on those days?

10. Are there certain times of day that the behavior is more or less likely to occur?

(Continued on next page.)

- If yes, what is going on in [   ]'s schedule at that time?

11. Are there certain settings in which the behavior is more or less likely to occur?

12. Are there certain people with whom the behavior is more or less likely to occur?

13. Are there certain activities during which the behavior is more or less likely to occur?

14. Are there certain materials that are usually present when the behavior occurs?

15. Are there certain materials that are usually not present when the behavior occurs?

    The task, when considering answers to all of the above, is to identify the variables that do and do not lead to the behavior. Think about the people who are around when the behavior occurs. What do they do differently than the people with whom the behavior does not occur? Do they offer a richer quality of attention when the child is on-task? Do they offer more consistent contingencies (i.e., reinforce-ent? punishment?) for inappropriate behavior? Alternatively, they may not place as many demands on the child. They may give her free access to preferred items or activities. Observations of each of these contrasts would lead you toward a different intervention.

    Sometimes differences in the child's behavior with different people are not due to these individuals' behaviors. Perhaps an instructor associated with greater behavior problems wears a certain perfume that the student attempts to escape from. Maybe one instructor's voice is louder than another's, which leads to the child's escape behaviors. In any case, you can see how identifying the specific variable associated with the behavior problem will guide intervention.

    Similarly, identifying specific environmental variables associated with the problem behavior will guide intervention. Consider lighting, smells, textures, tastes, temperature, crowded-ness, volume, etc. in each environment where the behavior does and does not occur. If you can isolate a variable that is common to settings where the behavior occurs and is absent from settings where the behavior does not occur, then you are on the path to effective intervention.

16. Have you noticed any common triggers for the behavior?
    Identifies immediate antecedents.

17. How do you usually respond to the behavior?
    Identifies consequences.

(Continued on next page.)

18. How do others usually respond to the behavior?
    Identifies consequences.

19. Do you think the behavior would happen if [   ] were
    left alone?

20. Have you ever walked in on [   ] performing the
    behavior when he or she was alone?
    *If the behavior occurs when the learner is left alone, this suggests
    automatically reinforced behavior—unless it occurs because no one is
    present to stop it (e.g., stealing cookies).*

Physiological Considerations

1. What medications is [   ] taking right now?

2. When did [   ] start taking this medication?

3. What are the possible side effects of this (these) medication(s)?

4. Why is he or she taking this medication?

5. Does [   ] have any illnesses or conditions?

    • If yes, do you notice any relationship between [   ]'s
      behavior and the severity of these conditions?

6. Describe [   ]'s sleep patterns.

    • Do you notice any relationship between [   ]'s
      sleep and behavior?

7. Describe [   ]'s eating patterns.

    • Do you notice any relationship between [   ]'s
      eating and behavior?

*These questions are geared toward assessing any physiological factors
affecting the behavior. These can either alter someone's threshold for
behavior—"shortening their fuse," so to speak, or may be associated
with automatic reinforcement behaviors. This information will also help
clarify whether or not a certain behavior problem may be a side effect
of a medication.*

SAMPLE
Functional Behavior Assessment Interview
for Students

Behavior: _____

Definition of Behavior: _____

_____

_____

_____

Date: _____
Interviewer (individual asking the questions): _____
Reporter (individual answering the questions): _____

[Interviewer: Adjust wording of questions according to child's age.]

1. When are you most likely to (problem behavior)? _____

_____

   a. Are there times that you are sure you would? _____

   b. Are there times that you are sure you wouldn't? _____

2. When is it the hardest to resist doing (problem behavior)?

_____

3. What could we do to help you not (problem behavior)?

_____

4. How do you let people know when something is too hard for you?

_____

   • How do they respond? _____

5. How do you let people know when something is too boring for you?

_____

   • How do they respond? _____

(Continued on next page.)

6. How do you let people know when you need a break?

_____

   • How do they respond? _____

7. How do you let people know when you need help?

_____

   • How do they respond? _____

8. How do you let people know when you need some attention?

_____

   • How do they respond? _____

9. How do you let people know when you need some space?

_____

   • How do they respond? _____

10. How do you let people know when you'd like to do a certain activity?

_____

   • How do they respond? _____

11. How does it feel to you when you do (problem behavior)?

_____

12. In general, would you describe your work as too hard, too easy, or just right?

_____

13. In general, do you feel that people notice when you do a good job?

_____

14. What are your favorite things to do? When do you get to do these?

_____

15. What are your least favorite things to do? When do you have to do these?

_____

16. Is there anything we could do to change your least favorite activities?

_____

6 | Observation Time

Up until this point, you have been gathering the tools that you'll need to investigate the seemingly senseless behavior of your child or student. Finally, you are ready to use these tools to investigate the behavior's function. Specifically, you will use systematic observation to try to identify MOs, immediate antecedents, and consequences that may be at play. This chapter will describe several approaches to observation commonly used in functional behavior assessments.

Step 7: Observe the Behavior

Listed below are several observational tools that can help unearth clues. You will not need to use all of these approaches in a single investigation. However, having information about each of them will allow you to choose one or more strategies to employ. Use the information from baseline and interviews to select when, where, and how to do your observation. For example, if interviews suggest that a child's behavior is very likely to occur on the school bus, then observing on the school bus is necessary. Similarly, if interviews suggest the behavior never occurs in the cafeteria, then an observation there is necessary as well to help you identify what conditions are in place in the cafeteria that are not in place on the bus.

Unstructured Observation

This approach is exactly what it sounds like: you take some time to pull yourself out of the situation and watch the behavior, along with its context. Stepping back in this way is critical because it is nearly impossible to get a clear picture of the influencing variables while interacting with your child or student.

While observing, ask yourself all of the questions included in the interview. For example, try to notice what happened just before the behavior and what happened just after the behavior. Try to identify what the child might have wanted, along with what he got. Make note of who is always around when the behavior occurs, and with whom the behavior is consistently absent. What do these individuals do differently with the child? Also notice during which activity the behavior occurs and which materials are being used at the time, as well as whether or not the context seems to affect the behavior.

Sometimes it is not possible to watch a child without altering his behavior (perhaps because he only does the behavior with you), or you may simply not have enough people around at the time that the behavior usually occurs to pull yourself away. If you are in this situation, consider setting up a video camera and trying to catch the behavior on tape. You can watch the tape later and get the same information from the video.

It is surprising how informative a simple peek at what is happening can be. Many times, patterns will jump out at you that will make the function of the behavior clear. For example, a behavior may occur consistently whenever a sibling enters the room. Or maybe the behavior occurs whenever it's time to put away a preferred activity. Sometimes a child will give you a clue while he is in the midst of the behavior, such as looking at someone's face for a certain response. Sometimes you might notice a consistent consequence. The more occurrences of the behavior you see, the more information you'll have. Try to see the behavior about ten times at a bare minimum, although guidelines for infrequent yet severe behaviors are presented later in the "Rare, but Dangerous Behaviors" section in Chapter 11 of this book.

Unstructured observation is a great way to develop hypotheses about the function of a behavior. You should spend some time doing unstructured observation as a first step in every functional behavior assessment. However, because there is no data collection to confirm or refute any hypotheses that develop, you must always use another observational strategy in conjunction with this one before completing your assessment.

Another tip you may find helpful in completing observations is to take note of what is going on with the child's peers. For example, if you observe at recess, and the child with ASD is wandering around without anything to do, look around and see if other children are doing the same. If so, the behaviors may say more about the setting or culture where you are observing than about the child, and your intervention should focus on altering that culture. Similarly, you may observe off-task behavior at a job site. While the individual you are observing may loaf a bit, if his coworkers are loafing too, it may be a by-product of that environment.

Structured Observation

In addition to using unstructured observation to gain information about the function of a behavior, it is often extremely useful to observe behavior very systematically. The main observation tools that are used for structured observations are:

- scatter plot data collection,
- A-B-C Data, and
- descriptive analysis.

Scatter Plot Data Collection

Scatter plots are a general data collection procedure developed by Paul E. Touchette (1985). The scatter plot is an interval recording method that allows you to determine whether a target behavior occurs during specific periods of time during the day. These data allow parents and practitioners to determine the extent to which the time of day affects the occurrence of the behavior you are observing. Scatter plot data are usually collected over a period of days or weeks until patterns of problem behavior emerge.

Scatter plots are generally represented in a grid format with interval blocks over the course of the day (see example below).

When completing the scatter plot, data collectors simply mark the block of time during which the target behavior occurred. There is no need to count instances of the behavior as you are focusing on the time of day during which problem behavior occurs.

In the example on page 83, intervals with episodes of problem behavior are shaded. You can see that, over the course of weeks, problem behavior most frequently occurs during weekdays between 9:00 a.m. and 10:00 a.m. and between 2:30 p.m. and 3:30 p.m. These results may suggest that the student has difficulties with transitions to and from school.

Sample Blank Scatter Plot

Start	End	M	T	W	TH	F	S	SU	M	T	W	TH	F	S	SU	M	T	W	TH	F	S	SU
8:00	8:30																					
8:30	9:00																					
9:00	9:30																					
9:30	10:00																					
10:00	10:30																					
10:30	11:00																					
11:00	11:30																					
11:30	12:00																					
12:00	12:30																					
12:30	1:00																					
1:00	1:30																					
1:30	2:00																					
2:00	2:30																					
2:30	3:00																					
3:00	3:30																					
3:30	4:00																					
4:00	4:30																					
4:30	5:00																					
5:00	5:30																					
5:30	6:00																					
6:00	6:30																					
6:30	7:00																					
7:00	7:30																					
7:30	8:00																					

Sample Scatter Plot of Problem Behaivor

Start	End	M	T	W	TH	F	S	SU	M	T	W	TH	F	S	SU	M	T	W	TH	F	S	SU
8:00	8:30																					
8:30	9:00																					
9:00	9:30	■			■	■					■	■	■				■	■	■	■		
9:30	10:00		■						■										■			
10:00	10:30																					
10:30	11:00																					
11:00	11:30												■									
11:30	12:00										■											
12:00	12:30			■																		
12:30	1:00																					
1:00	1:30							■													■	
1:30	2:00																					
2:00	2:30																					
2:30	3:00				■					■						■						
3:00	3:30	■		■		■			■				■									
3:30	4:00																					
4:00	4:30														■							
4:30	5:00																					
5:00	5:30													■								
5:30	6:00																					
6:00	6:30																					
6:30	7:00																					
7:00	7:30																					
7:30	8:00																					

Scatter plots are useful tools for gathering information about environmental events that may trigger episodes of problem behavior. They do not necessarily provide information about specific antecedents that cause problem behavior, but they provide useful information about the environment in which problem behavior occurs.

A-B-C Data

"A-B-C" data stands for "Antecedent-Behavior-Consequence." As you might guess, the purpose of identifying A-B-C patterns is to develop hypotheses about what exactly has been learned about the problem behavior. We can identify the behavior's function by identifying consequences that reverse antecedents (e.g., A = teacher walks away from student, B = problem behavior, C = teacher returns to student to redirect him). Similarly, by identifying consistent pairings between antecedents and consequences, we might identify events that act as S^Ds for the behavior. For example, imagine a child who always cries for candy when his grandmother comes over and then is given some candy. For this child, Grandma may be an S^D signaling the availability of candy. Consider the following examples on the chart on page 85 and then try to complete the blank spaces in the chart on your own.

Notice in the above examples that each antecedent is a discrete event. The immediate antecedent is whatever changed in the environment just as the behavior occurred. These events may either trigger EOs or serve as S^Ds for the problem behavior.

Individuals new to A-B-C data collection commonly make the mistake of describing a setting or ongoing activity rather than identifying an antecedent. For example, for number 5, if the antecedent had been listed as "play with Mom," the function of the behavior would have been less clear. For number 1, if the antecedent had been listed as "classroom," again the function of the behavior would have been less clear. It is sometimes challenging to identify relevant discrete changes in the environment that precede a behavior, but doing so will lead to much clearer assessment information. With practice, identifying these discrete antecedents becomes easier.

To help the observer distinguish between settings, ongoing activities, and immediate antecedents, each of these categories are included on the A-B-C Data Sheet in Appendix G. This sheet has the format of a checklist with prewritten categories so that the data collector need only mark a box. This is often helpful when asking people

Examples of Antecedents, Behaviors & Consequences with Possible Functions

Example Number	Antecedent	Behavior	Consequence	Possible function(s)
1	"Time for work"	Mia pounds her fist on her desk	Time out in hallway	Escape task
2	Peer approach and greeting	Mia pounds her fist on her desk	Peer walks away	Escape peer interaction
3	Alone, no demands, no specific activity	Mia pounds her fist on her desk	Alone, no demands, no specific activity	Automatic reinforcement
4	Alone, no demands, no specific activity	Mia pounds her fist on her desk	Sent for therapeutic brushing	Automatic reinforcement; access to brushing
5	Mom interrupts play with Mia to answer ringing phone	Mia pounds her fist on her desk	Mom hangs up to attend to problem behavior	Obtain attention
6	Peer greets another peer	Mia pounds her fist on her desk	Peers laugh and smile at Mia	
7	Instructor says, "Do this" and presents model for imitation	Mia pounds her fist on her desk	Instructor restrains Mia	
8	Dad shuts light, says "good night"	Mia pounds her fist on her desk	Mia alone in room in dark	

Answers:

6. Obtain peer attention

7. Escape task; obtain physical attention

8. Automatic reinforcement

who are newer to the process collect ABC data. By creating predefined categories that need only to be checked, we take the judgment out of deciding what should be recorded and what should be omitted. As a result, data can be collected by those with less experience or training. As an added bonus, this checklist format saves the time involved in writing, allowing for closer observations.

While our example provides a sample that may be useful to you, feel free to create your own form with customized categories for your unique needs.

ABC DATA SHEET   **Date:**

Date/ Time	Setting	Antecedents	Behavior	Consequence
	❑ Homework ❑ Leisure ❑ Meal ❑ Other _____	❑ Work Presented ❑ Error Correction ❑ Told "No" ❑ Stop a Preferred Activity ❑ No One Attending to Him ❑ Transition ❑ Other _____	❑ Inapp. Vocal ❑ Aggression ❑ Disruption ❑ Tantrum ❑ Other _____	❑ Reprimand/Talk to Him ❑ Ignore Him ❑ Break from Work/Back Off ❑ Make Him Work ❑ Deny Access ❑ Other _____
	❑ Homework ❑ Leisure ❑ Meal ❑ Other _____	❑ Work Presented ❑ Error Correction ❑ Told "No" ❑ Stop a Preferred Activity ❑ No One Attending to Him ❑ Transition ❑ Other _____	❑ Inapp. Vocal ❑ Aggression ❑ Disruption ❑ Tantrum ❑ Other _____	❑ Reprimand/Talk to Him ❑ Ignore Him ❑ Break from Work/Back Off ❑ Make Him Work ❑ Deny Access ❑ Other _____
	❑ Homework ❑ Leisure ❑ Meal ❑ Other _____	❑ Work Presented ❑ Error Correction ❑ Told "No" ❑ Stop a Preferred Activity ❑ No One Attending to Him ❑ Transition ❑ Other _____	❑ Inapp. Vocal ❑ Aggression ❑ Disruption ❑ Tantrum ❑ Other _____	❑ Reprimand/Talk to Him ❑ Ignore Him ❑ Break from Work/Back Off ❑ Make Him Work ❑ Deny Access ❑ Other _____
	❑ Homework ❑ Leisure ❑ Meal ❑ Other _____	❑ Work Presented ❑ Error Correction ❑ Told "No" ❑ Stop a Preferred Activity ❑ No One Attending to Him ❑ Transition ❑ Other _____	❑ Inapp. Vocal ❑ Aggression ❑ Disruption ❑ Tantrum ❑ Other _____	❑ Reprimand/Talk to Him ❑ Ignore Him ❑ Break from Work/Back Off ❑ Make Him Work ❑ Deny Access ❑ Other _____
	❑ Homework ❑ Leisure ❑ Meal ❑ Other _____	❑ Work Presented ❑ Error Correction ❑ Told "No" ❑ Stop a Preferred Activity ❑ No One Attending to Him ❑ Transition ❑ Other _____	❑ Inapp. Vocal ❑ Aggression ❑ Disruption ❑ Tantrum ❑ Other _____	❑ Reprimand/Talk to Him ❑ Ignore Him ❑ Break from Work/Back Off ❑ Make Him Work ❑ Deny Access ❑ Other _____

Another error that individuals who are new to A-B-C data often make is to draw conclusions from too few A-B-C sequences. To suggest that a behavior has a certain function, A-B-C data need to show a pattern repeatedly. To help identify predominant patterns in your A-B-C data, you will be asked to total the number of times that each possible function arises at the bottom of your data sheet. If one possible function emerges much more often than others, you have some evidence to suggest that it might be influencing the behavior.

If possible, try to have more than one person collect A-B-C data and also evaluate the data as to possible functions. Unfortunately, recent research findings suggest that different raters of A-B-C data do not always agree with one another (Kwak, Ervin, Anderson & Austin, 2004). This tells us that the same set of data may be interpreted differently by different raters. If you can have another person review your data, and your ratings agree, this makes your findings particularly compelling. Nevertheless, it will still be best to try to confirm these findings through another observation method.

ABC Quadrant Analysis: One method of analysis of ABC data that we use with our clients is called ABC Quadrant Analysis (ABC-QA). Using this method, we systematically assess what exactly changed in the individual's environment as a result of the behavior. By calculating how often certain changes in the environment co-occur with the problem behavior, we learn about the likely function. We are in the process of studying this method experimentally to document whether it actually makes it easier for multiple raters to agree and whether the outcomes are closer to what we find with experimental measures.

When using ABC-QA, choose one possible function of the behavior. Let's use attention as an example. Then, draw a table with four quadrants (or sections) related to attention. Indicate what was in place for the learner with regard to attention before and after the behavior. See our example below:

Did the child have the type of attention being studied (e.g., intense physical attention)?

	Yes, before the behavior	No, before the behavior
Yes, after the behavior	Quadrant #1	Quadrant #2
No, after the behavior	Quadrant # 3	Quadrant #4

Take the ABC data you collected and plot it into these quadrants for one possible function at a time. For example, using the sample data on page 85 for Mia, in the first event, Mia had attention before the behavior (the teacher placed a demand) but not after (alone in time-out). Therefore a hash mark would be written in quadrant 3. In the second event, Mia again had attention before the behavior (peer greeted) but not after (peer walked away). Another hash mark would be placed in quadrant 3. If the remainder of the data showed a pattern of most responses falling in quadrant 3, we might suspect that Mia uses the challenging behaviors to escape interactions with others.

In contrast, if the majority of the instances of the behavior you observed fell into quadrants 1 or 4, then attention was not likely the function of the behavior. If the majority of your instances of the behavior fell into quadrant 2, it is likely that the behavior helps the individual gain attention, such as a child who raises a ruckus whenever his parent gets on the phone.

	Yes, before the behavior	No, before the behavior
Yes, after the behavior	Quadrant #1 I	Quadrant #2
No, after the behavior	Quadrant # 3 卄卄	Quadrant #4 II

Descriptive Analysis

A descriptive analysis involves comparing the strength of the behavior under different naturally occurring conditions. Using this method requires the observer to quickly recognize the controlling factors in place. The observer must be able to identify the answers to each of the following questions on a moment-to-moment basis:

1. Is there a demand on the individual?
2. Is he receiving attention?
3. Is his access to a desired item or activity restricted?

It may be helpful to use your knowledge of the child's daily routine to try to plan times to observe under four conditions:

1. high demands,
2. low attention,

3. restricted access to things he likes, and
4. free access to preferred items and attention.

If this is not possible, don't worry. You can also watch any time and sort out which of the above conditions were in place.

Sometimes the situations that you'd like to observe (i.e., low attention, high demands, and restricted access) do not occur naturally. If so, you may have to ask the adult who will be interacting with the child to set these situations up. However, keep in mind that this does not guarantee that those conditions will be in place. For example, you may ask a teacher to place demands on a student, but the demands might get derailed by off-task behavior. Or an adult may provide constant eye contact to a student she is supposed to be ignoring.

These observations provide extremely valuable information for your assessment regarding both the impact of the child's behavior on his environment and the way that others in that environment respond to him. Observe and decide what conditions are in place.

The observer then uses his or her measurement tools to record the strength of the behavior under each condition. (Refer back to Chapter 4 for information on measuring behaviors.) By calculating the average strength of the behavior under each condition, the observer gathers evidence as to what the function(s) of the behavior might be. For example, if a behavior is much more likely to occur when someone places a particular type of demand on the individual, then the behavior likely serves as an escape from that particular type of demand. If the behavior occurs more frequently when the individual is not receiving attention, then the behavior may function to obtain attention. If the behavior occurs whenever the individual's access to a desired item is restricted, then the behavior may operate to get the item back.

When interpreting your data, you can calculate what are referred to as *conditional probabilities.* To calculate conditional probabilities, you first count the total number of episodes of problem behavior. Then you calculate the probability that specific antecedents and consequences precede or follow episodes of problem behavior. For example, imagine that you observed twenty episodes of a behavior. Fifteen of these episodes were preceded by demands made on the individual, and four were preceded by restricted access to preferred items/activities. The conditional probability of demand presentation preceding problem behavior would be 75 percent (15 divided by 20). The conditional probability for restricted access preceding problem behavior would be

20 percent (4 divided by 20). Calculating the conditional probabilities for the consequences is done in a similar way. For example, assume that fourteen of those twenty episodes were followed by a brief break in demands. That means the conditional probability of a break occurring as a consequence of the behavior is 70 percent (14 divided by 20).

Sometimes, a given behavior occurs fairly equally across all conditions. In this case, either the behavior actually serves each function, or the behavior is automatically reinforcing for the person. To help flesh this out, try observing the individual when he is alone. If the behavior often occurs when he is alone, there is a good chance that the behavior serves an automatic reinforcement function. Nothing in the external environment is changing, but the behavior occurs anyway. Immediate antecedents and reinforcers for the behavior are taking place internally. Alternatively, if the behavior does not occur when your child or student is alone, consider his communication skills and whether his appropriate requests are being reinforced.

If the individual's communication skills need to be developed, and/or his appropriate requests are unlikely to be reinforced, then it is likely that the seemingly senseless behavior actually serves multiple functions.

In order to simplify the observation and interpretation process, a Descriptive Analysis Data Sheet is included in Appendix H.

7 | Test Your Hypothesis

After using the observational methods described in the previous chapter, you will have some hypotheses, or informed guesses, about the function of your child's or student's behavior. Now is the time to test your hypotheses to see whether you are correct. To accurately test your hypotheses, you can make changes to the environment to see what "turns the behavior on" and "turns the behavior off." This chapter describes systematic scientific procedures designed to help you isolate variables that may be contributing to behavior problems. With these strategies, you will not just record and categorize naturally occurring behavior, you will actually attempt to evoke the problem behavior, and, in some cases, reinforce it.

For less complex behaviors, it is usually sufficient to try to use *antecedent manipulations* first (see below). This assessment approach is easier to implement correctly, can be completed quickly, and will provide sufficient information to address most behavior problems. For more complex behaviors, a *functional analysis* may be warranted. This is the "gold standard" of assessment tools and can help shed light on even the most puzzling behavior problems. However, as this is more complicated and requires evoking and reinforcing more of the challenging behavior, you may need the help of a professional to implement this approach, at least the first couple of times that you use it.

Importantly, before you use any of the techniques described that involve evoking the behavior (i.e., setting up scenarios in which the behavior is likely to occur), consider the safety of everyone involved. Do not trigger dangerous behaviors without taking any necessary precautions first. For example, you may need something as intensive as asking a professional trained in crisis management to be present, or you may need something as simple as having the parent sit near the door so that a quick exit is possible if behaviors escalate.

Prior to Starting Hypothesis Testing

Although it is often tempting to "jump right in" when testing your hypotheses, it is important that you take some steps to prepare for the process. Being prepared will increase the likelihood of success.

Get Some Help: Conducting antecedent manipulations and functional analyses can be difficult to do alone. You should use the team that you assembled at the start of the assessment process to help you design and conduct your tests. This can include a consultant, a child study team member, or classroom staff. Hypothesis testing is best conducted with a group to bounce ideas off of and to serve as peers to review your ideas.

Get Consent: Prior to implementing any kind of systematic assessment, you will need to obtain written consent from the relevant guardians. You should not conduct antecedent manipulations or functional analysis without permission. A consent form should include a description of the procedures that you will be using. (See Appendix I for an example of a consent form.)

Use Your Observation Data: To help to design your conditions, use what you learned from your observations to decide on specifics. For example, you may be able to identify demands that are difficult for the person or stimuli that she finds aversive. You can then test whether or not she uses problem behaviors to escape demands. It can also help to identify types of attention (e.g., reprimands, soothing comments, physical contact) or tangible items the individual prefers when you are testing whether or not problem behaviors occur to obtain attention.

Design Your Conditions and Write Down the Procedures: After you have done some observation, you should be ready to design your conditions. When designing your conditions, it is important to make them as representative of the natural environment as possible. This will prevent the individual from identifying this as a new situation and changing his or her behavior. For example, if the behavior usually occurs during math and math is always right after lunch, don't suddenly start working on math first thing in the morning. Or don't have a completely different instructor teaching math in a completely different room if it can be avoided.

You can then select the length of the conditions. As a general rule, if problem behavior happens frequently (e.g., several times a minute) you can use shorter sessions. If problem behavior occurs at a low frequency, sessions/observations may have to be longer to capture the problem effectively.

Once you have determined your design, you should write down what your procedures will look like. This will be helpful because it will allow you to explain the procedures to others after the assessment is complete, provide appropriate documentation, and help to inform future analyses, if necessary.

Antecedent Manipulations

Like descriptive analysis, discussed in Chapter 6, antecedent manipulation involves comparing the strength of the behavior under different environmental conditions. However, in contrast to descriptive analysis, antecedent manipulation involves contriving situations to observe rather than waiting for events to take place naturally. Therefore, to use antecedent manipulation, the observer must actively set up different conditions to evaluate.

When using antecedent manipulations, you can test any hypotheses that you have developed during unstructured observation or descriptive analysis. Simply put, you expose the person to different conditions or situations and see if the problem behavior occurs. There is no systematic response to target behavior when using antecedent manipulations. When using these procedures, it is important to set up conditions in which problem behavior is *likely to occur* and when it is *unlikely to occur*. Conditions you may set up include:

1. *Little or no attention:* In this condition, you engage the individual in a preferred type of interaction (e.g., peek-a-boo, tickling, a conversation, etc.) and then step away from her or start interacting with another person (divided attention). It is important to verify the type of attention the individual prefers (e.g., talking about preferred topics, physical attention).

2. *Restricted access*: In this condition, you withhold access to highly preferred items or activities (e.g., turning off a preferred video, not allowing the person to play a game on the computer, taking away a preferred toy). In some cases, the activity that is restricted may be a behavior (e.g., lining up objects, self-talk).
3. *Aversive stimulation*: In this condition, you engage the individual in nonpreferred activities (e.g., academic demands, social demands, noise, exposure to specific people).

Whatever conditions you choose to test, you will also want to include "control" conditions. These "control" conditions provide a contrast to the other conditions. In other words, you want to design conditions where you are *unlikely* to see the problem behavior.

1. *High levels of attention*: During this condition, you provide access to preferred forms of attention (e.g., talking to the person, reprimands, physical contact).
2. *Access to objects and/or activities*: In this condition, you allow the individual to have free access to preferred items, activities, or behavior.
3. *No aversive stimulation*: In this condition, you ensure that the individual can avoid any aversive stimulation (e.g., academics, social demands, noise, or specific people). This is functionally a break.

Data Collection and Interpretation: Below is an example of a completed antecedent manipulation, or "AB functional analysis," data sheet. (A blank copy of this data sheet and an alternative data sheet for assessing the effects of antecedent manipulations can be found in Appendices J and K.) For each contrived situation (e.g., attention, no attention), you tally the amount of target behavior occurring during each session. For example, in the data sheet below, you will see that there were ten minutes during which we ensured that the learner had high rates of attention. During those ten minutes, the behavior occurred five times. In contrast, the student had *no* attention for ten minutes later on, and the behavior occurred four times. This is not a very big contrast. However, there was a very big difference between how often the behavior occurred when the student had ten minutes without access to his preferred things (forty-three times) versus when he did have access to his preferred things (eight times).

There will be times when you cannot control the exact length of a condition. In the example below, maybe the task we were interested in seeing the student complete takes twenty minutes to complete. By recording the time, we can then convert what we find to rate per minute to allow sessions of one duration to be compared with sessions of a different duration. For the "work" versus "no work" comparison, we are not comparing fourteen instances of the behavior to four instances of the behavior—this would make no sense, as we would expect more instances of the behavior to occur across more time (twenty minutes versus ten minutes). We would divide 14 by 20 to get a rate of .7 behaviors per minute during work and compare that to .4 (4 instances divided by 10 minutes). Multiple observations should be conducted for each condition.

AB Functional Analysis Data Sheet

Time	Attention	No Attention	Access to Preferred Items and Activities	No Access to Preferred Items and Activities	Work	No Work
10 minutes	5					
10 minutes						4
20 minutes					14	
10 minutes	4					
10 minutes			8			
10 minutes				43		

These numbers can then be graphed in a bar graph to allow for easy interpretation, as shown on the next page.

The summarized data in this graph suggest that problem behavior occurs at a high rate when the individual's access to preferred items/activities is restricted. This hypothesis is strengthened by the fact that problem behavior occurs at low rates when the person has access to preferred items.

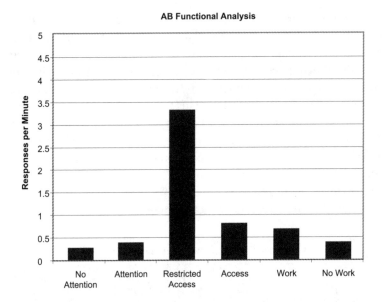

Antecedent manipulations are a useful tool when testing your hypothesis about the function of an individual's problem behavior. It gives you more control than you have when using descriptive assessment techniques, which allows you to be more confident that you have identified the function of the behavior.

Functional Analysis

The most sophisticated procedure in the functional assessment hierarchy is functional analysis. When conducting a functional analysis, both antecedents (the environment prior to problem behavior) and consequences (how you respond to problem behavior) are manipulated to see when the target behavior is most likely to occur. When conducting a functional analysis, you are designing conditions or settings that mimic what occurs in the natural environment. However, unlike what happens in the natural environment, you test one variable at a time during a functional analysis. For example, if the hypothesis is that your child or student is engaging in aggression because she wants attention, you should provide attention following aggression. That way you can see if aggression occurs more frequently than in conditions during which she has free access to attention (i.e., the control/toy play condition, discussed below).

Functional Analysis Conditions

While functional analysis conditions are tailored to meet the needs of individuals, there are five conditions that are most commonly used. Two of the conditions test for consequences that are delivered to the person: 1) attention, and 2) preferred items and activities. A third condition tests for consequences that involve removing something, such as work or social demands. The fourth condition, in which the individual is left alone or ignored, is a test for automatic reinforcement. Finally, a "control" condition is designed to provide a contrast to the other conditions. It is meant to be a condition where you are unlikely to see the problem behavior.

A more detailed description of how these conditions look is presented below.

Attention Condition

Prior to testing the attention condition, you typically provide preferred forms of attention (verbal/physical attention) for one or two minutes to ensure that the individual is eager for your attention. Then, at the start of the session, you act distracted (e.g., reading a book, holding a phone to your ear). When the problem behavior occurs, you interact with your child or student for twenty to thirty seconds (e.g., "Don't hit me!" or "Why are you hitting your head!").

The person who is observing and recording the data should do so as covertly as possible. Try to watch out of the corner of your eye or to immediately look away if the person sees you watching her. If there is a window or television on in the room, you might try to position yourself so that it appears that you are looking out the window or watching television, when you can, in fact, see the child from that angle. Be sure that during this observation there are no demands on the child and that she has access to many preferred objects and activities. This allows you to control for other motivations to some degree.

If high rates of the behavior occur in this condition relative to the control condition (see below), the behavior may serve to obtain attention for the individual.

Tangible Condition

Prior to the start of the tangible condition, the examiner provides access to highly preferred items or activities for one or two minutes.

As your child or student becomes interested in one, take it away. If possible, leave it where she can see it, but out of her reach. Announce that it is out of batteries, or too noisy, or that for some reason you want to save it for later. All the while that the desired item is out of reach, provide a rich level of attention and no demands. This will control for other motivations to some degree.

While some people—with and without an ASD—will wait patiently for the item and instead find another item or engage in some social interaction, others will launch into a problem behavior to try to get the toy. If your child or student uses a problem behavior as a means of accessing preferred objects and activities, you can expect to see her display the problem behavior in an attempt to get the removed item back. If she does engage in the problem behavior, give the item back for a period of twenty to thirty seconds.

Higher rates of the problem behavior in this condition compared to the control condition indicate that the person's problem behavior is maintained by access to tangible items.

Demand Condition

In the demand condition, you present difficult academic demands to the student (e.g., writing tasks, fine motor activities), or other demands that she finds aversive (e.g., cleaning, self-care, etc.). If your observational data indicate that she could be using the problem behavior to avoid something in particular (e.g., nonpreferred foods, noise), use that stimulus for this condition.

At the start of the demand session, you begin presenting demands. Once the problem behavior occurs, you remove demands for about twenty to thirty seconds. High rates of problem behavior in this condition relative to the control condition suggest that escape from demands functions as a reinforcement for the problem behavior.

Alone/Ignore Condition

If a behavior is automatically reinforcing, then the person is not trying to give anyone a message through her behavior. Therefore, she may frequently engage in it when she is alone and does not have other things to do. Either use a video camera or stand outside the room and try to watch the person without being seen. Make sure she does not have any objects or activities nearby to fill her time. Do not enter the room or allow yourself to be seen unless it is necessary to preserve safety.

This assessment is not appropriate for children with very dangerous behavior problems, for very young children, or for others who would not ordinarily be left alone in a room.

The key is to leave the individual with nothing really to do, and see how she entertains herself. Some people might hum or sing songs, and others might engage in the challenging behavior. To make this condition less artificial, you can introduce it to the individual as a "waiting" condition. Let her know that you are going to go get something and that you'll be right back. This type of condition may evoke behaviors that occur as a result of the person being "bored."

If there are concerns that the behavior is dangerous and may need to be interrupted, you can test this condition when you are present but do not interact with the individual (i.e., ignore her). High rates of target behavior in this condition may suggest that the behavior is maintained by the natural consequences that the behavior itself produces (e.g., sensory stimulation).

Control Condition

The *control* condition is the control to which all other conditions are compared. The individual is placed in an "enriched environment" where she has access to preferred items, as much attention as she would like, and no demands or aversive stimulation. In other words, the environment should be set up so it is unlikely to evoke the challenging behavior. In this condition, the examiner does not modify his behavior if the problem behavior occurs. Low rates of the behavior are expected in this condition.

The traditional functional analysis conditions are summarized in the table on the next page.

Using Cues to Signal Conditions

Each hypothesis-testing condition should be associated with a certain cue, if possible. This may help your child or student recognize the condition during subsequent testing sessions and possibly engage in the problem behaviors more quickly. Cues you might consider include running different conditions in different rooms, draping different brightly colored towels over the couch for different sessions, or having the child sit in a different part of a room in different conditions. For example, if you are only comparing two conditions, you might leave the

Functional Analysis Conditions

Conditions	Just Before the Session Begins	Start of the Session/ Antecedent Condition	What Happens When Target Behavior Occurs
Social Attention Condition	Free access to attention (physical or verbal)	Therapist pretends to be distracted (e.g., reading)	20–30 seconds of attention (e.g., reprimands, asking what is wrong)
Tangible Condition	Free access to highly preferred activities	Access to preferred items/activities withheld	20–30 seconds of access (e.g., video turned on, toys provided)
Demand Condition	n/a	Aversive stimuli presented (e.g., difficult academic demands, noise)	20–30 seconds of escape (e.g., academic materials removed)
Alone/Ignore Condition	n/a	Individual is left alone in a room (or adult is present, but does not interact).	No response to target behavior
Control	n/a	Individual has access to high preference items and attention. No demands presented.	No response to target behavior

drapes open during one condition and closed during another. If your child is not happy with the arrangement (for example, asks to open drapes that are closed), you'll have to grant her request. Otherwise, you will create an unintentional restricted access condition (e.g., restricted access to looking out of the window).

If your child asks why the unusual item is placed where it is or the way it is, you can try to link it to whatever condition you are contriving. If you are about to do a low attention condition, for example, you can say that you've thrown a blanket over the couch because you are going to snuggle up in it while you read a book. If you are about to do a restricted access condition, you can explain that you put the blanket there so that you can keep her toy on it while it waits for new batteries.

Taking Safety Precautions

A special concern to think through before using antecedent manipulations or any other strategy that may bring out the challenging behavior, such as functional analysis, is that you are essentially trying to evoke the problem behavior. Figuring out how you evoke it will let you know the behavior's function. However, for severe or dangerous behaviors, you must determine whether or not the benefits of conducting the assessment outweigh the risks of the behavior itself. For example, you may have a student who bangs her head and want to determine why. But if the head-banging episodes result in bruising or other serious injuries, it may be best to avoid this type of assessment if you do not have special mats or other precautions that would ensure her safety.

Always have a safety plan in case a behavior escalates under these conditions. You may want to have a safe place to direct the child to where she cannot hurt herself and can calm down. You may also want to have known distractors available if you need to end the assessment early. Protective gear, such as arm-pads or helmets, may be needed to prevent injury if a behavior escalates. It may also be wise to try to complete the assessment at a time when no other children are around. Finally, you may want a team member who knows how to use physical restraint present.

Many individuals with autism spectrum disorders do not have extensive exposure to the conditions that evoke their problem behavior in everyday life because as soon as they engage in the behavior, people take steps to get them to stop before anyone is hurt. They may get a small dose of the condition and begin the problem behavior, and the condition ends. Because the goal of both antecedent manipulation and functional analysis is for the person to spend a certain period of time under these conditions, the condition is continually reintroduced until the goal time is met. This might involve more exposure to these conditions than the individual is used to. As a consequence, she may exhibit the behavior problem to a more intense degree. Keep this risk in mind as you decide whether or not to use these strategies.

Analyzing Your Data

After you have completed one round of *antecedent manipulations,* you should optimally repeat these conditions one or two more times to ensure that consistent patterns emerge. You should also prioritize safety when deciding how many times to repeat the conditions.

When conducting a *functional analysis,* several series of these conditions are usually run until a clear pattern is discerned. In most cases, functional analyses are conducted using a "multi-element research design." Multi-element designs involve running each condition in a series (e.g., attention, tangible, alone, demand, toy play), and then repeating the series until a pattern is determined. Furthermore, graphing the information you collect is critical here. Visually analyzing the data will help you to identify the function of the problem behavior. The best way to interpret a functional analysis graph is to determine which conditions are the most different in level from the control condition.

You can use the blank Functional Analysis Data Sheet (Appendix L) to collect data on how often a problem behavior occurs in each condition. Below is a data sheet that has been filled out showing a clear difference in level for the demand condition.

Functional Analysis Data Sheet

	Series 1	Series 2	Series 3	Series 4	Series 5
Attention	0	II	0	0	0
Demand	⊬Ħ	⊬Ħ ⊬Ħ	⊬Ħ IIII	⊬Ħ II	⊬Ħ III
Tangible	0	0	I	I	0
Alone	I	0	0	0	0
Play	0	0	0	0	0

On the next page is an example of a graph of a functional analysis. In the graph, it is clear that the individual has high levels of problematic behavior in the low attention condition (represented by the open squares) relative to the play or control condition, in which she has all of his preferred things as well as attention and no demands (represented by the filled circles). These findings clearly suggest that the problem behavior serves an attention function.

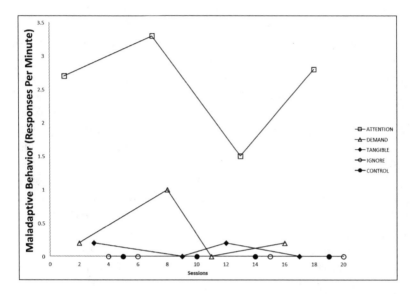

Below is another example of a graph of a functional analysis. In this analysis, the only condition in which maladaptive behavior was observed was the demand condition. The fact that problem behavior occurs in when demands are presented and not in the control condition suggests an escape function.

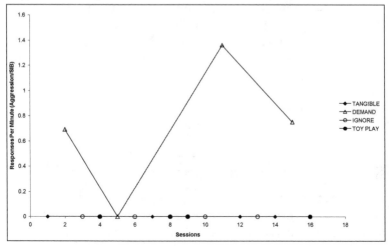

Why Is Functional Analysis Worthwhile?

You might wonder how any good at all can come of reinforcing a problem behavior. First, as discussed in our review of the research of Iwata and colleagues (1982/1994), reinforcing a behavior gives us an opportunity to reenact events that occur in the person's everyday life. We can see which consequence has the power to strengthen the behavior within controlled sessions. This gives us a good idea of what consequences are maintaining the behavior outside of sessions (e.g., at home, in the classroom).

Some people voice concerns that a functional analysis will teach an individual that her inappropriate behavior is an effective method of communication and that she will have to "unlearn" this after the assessment process. While it may seem counterintuitive, exposing someone with an ASD to a functional analysis might actually help her to unlearn a behavior more quickly. In everyday life, problem behaviors are usually reinforced inconsistently. Children with ASD never know which instance of their behavior will be reinforced. Therefore, if at first they don't succeed, they keep trying. Like gamblers playing a slot machine, they learn to persist in the behavior.

In contrast, during the assessment process, each instance of problem behavior is getting reinforced. This continuous pattern of reinforcement actually teaches people with ASD to be less persistent. For example, every time you pick up your telephone, there is a dial tone. You are continually reinforced for picking up your phone. If there suddenly is no dial tone, after a brief bout of trying to identify the problem, you will give up and declare the phone dead. This is what we want to happen to individuals with challenging behavior. If we take a behavior out of the intermittent reinforcement schedule that it receives in everyday life, and place it on the continuous schedule that it receives during a functional analysis, then the behavior may actually persist for less time during intervention.

Brief Models of Functional Analysis

One of the main criticisms of functional analyses is the amount of time required to conduct them. Indeed, when run in the traditional format (each session lasting fifteen minutes), the amount of session time can make using such procedures prohibitive. However, the literature suggests that shorter functional analyses can yield similar results to longer models.

In a study conducted by M. D. Wallace and Brian Iwata (1999), the authors found that five- or ten-minute FA sessions can yield similar results to fifteen-minute FA sessions. In the study, the authors studied data from functional analyses using fifteen-minute sessions. The raters then coded the first ten minutes of the fifteen-minute sessions, graphed the data, and looked for a relationship between the patterns that they found and those that emerged using data from all fifteen minutes. They then coded only the first five minutes of the fifteen-minutes sessions, graphed the data, and looked for a relationship between the patterns for this slice of the assessment versus the whole. The authors found that ten-minute sessions and fifteen-minute sessions corresponded perfectly (forty-six out of forty-six cases). In addition, they found that five-minute sessions corresponded with fifteen-minute sessions 93.5 percent of the time (forty-three out of forty-six cases). These findings suggest that you can run five- or ten-minute FA sessions, which can reduce session time considerably.

Another shortcut you may consider is a *hypothesis-driven functional analysis.* In earlier phases of the assessment, you may be able to rule out certain functions for challenging behavior. For example, in most cases physical aggression is not automatically reinforced (with some exceptions). Therefore, unless you have reason to believe that aggression is maintained by automatic reinforcement, you can eliminate the alone condition from your functional analysis. You might encounter a student who actively avoids social interaction during all of your observations. In such a circumstance, you may be able to eliminate the social attention condition from your FA. By running fewer session types (three or four session types, rather than five), hypothesis-driven FAs can reduce session time considerably.

Conclusion

Functional analyses are the gold standard of functional assessment. Results of a functional analysis are typically considered to be the most valid of any assessment tool. Volumes of research attest to the effectiveness of functional analysis in finding the communicative message of a person's behavior and in leading to successful interventions. However, FAs are labor intensive and involve certain risks. Consequently, it may be best to reserve this strategy for exceptionally confusing behaviors for which other assessment approaches have failed. Additionally, because this approach involves evoking and temporarily strengthening the problem behavior, it is best if only experienced professionals conduct functional analyses for very severe or dangerous behaviors. Furthermore, they should conduct their analyses in highly controlled settings.

There are inpatient placements available where functional analyses of even the most severe behavior problems can be implemented by teams of experts with the training and resources to preserve the safety of the person with ASD and themselves. If you are faced with a problem behavior that is extremely dangerous or destructive, or that has been unsuccessfully addressed by a skilled behavior analyst on an outpatient basis, consider an inpatient placement. The length of stay can vary from a few weeks to several months, depending on how long it takes to identify distinct patterns of the behavior under different conditions. To find a local setting that can provide this type of service, check the Behavior Analyst Certification Board's website (www.bacb.com) and contact a local board-certified practitioner. He or she should be able to direct you to an appropriate provider.

8 | Alternative Assessment Models

As noted in the previous chapter, functional analyses represent the most *empirically sound* (proven by research) assessment procedures for identifying why problem behavior occurs (e.g., to get attention, to escape demands). In most cases, the advantages of functional analysis far outweigh any disadvantages. Hundreds of well-designed research studies have confirmed the usefulness of functional analyses, and these procedures have led to improved outcomes for countless individuals with behavioral difficulties. However, practitioners often encounter challenges when trying to implement traditional FA procedures in real-life settings. The most commonly reported hurdles include 1) lack of resources to maintain safety and collect the data correctly and 2) ethical concerns from parents, teachers, and other laymen about reinforcing dangerous behaviors.

When implemented in a traditional format, functional analyses can be time-consuming and put a strain on available resources. Generally speaking, conducting a sound functional analysis requires a team. In a financial climate in which school districts are struggling to provide needed services with fewer and fewer resources, schools may not be able to afford a full functional analysis for every student who could benefit from one. Unfortunately, the end result is that practitioners use less precise assessment tools and make more errors in treatment selection, so behavior problems aren't resolved as well as they could be. And ultimately, this may end up costing them more in terms of time and money.

In addition to these practical constraints, functional analysis can raise ethical concerns. Traditional models of functional analysis require that the problem behavior be reinforced. In most cases, briefly reinforc-ing a target behavior to identify the function is appropriate. After all, the problem behavior is receiving reinforcement in the natural environment anyway. But even though it is very important to see the circumstances under which problem behavior occurs, this exposes the student and the therapist to potentially dangerous behavior that may result in injury to either party (e.g., aggression or self-injurious behavior).

Another concern is the use of functional analysis for low-frequen-cy problem behavior (e.g., behavior that occurs once a week or once a month). Conducting FAs for low-frequency behavior can be particularly challenging, as the behavior generally has to occur at a fairly high rate (at least once every five or ten minutes) to yield results that can be interpreted. Here again, it may be questionable as to whether evok-ing infrequent problem behavior is ethical. For example, if a student engaged in a dangerous form of problem behavior once every two or three weeks, would it be ethical for you to evoke the behavior dozens of times per hour for the purpose of assessment?

Limited resources, risk of injury, and the evocation of danger-ous behavior present challenges for practitioners when conducting functional analyses. Therefore, despite the effectiveness of functional analysis procedures for identifying the functions of challenging be-havior so that effective intervention plans can be developed, modi-fications may be required in specific instances. These modifications can allow you to minimize the impact of problem behavior and lessen the risk of injury.

Alternative Assessment Models

To address some of these practical and ethical issues related to functional analyses, some alternative models of assessment have been developed. These alternative models include the following:

- *trial-based functional analyses* (Bloom, Iwata, Fritz, Roscoe & Carreau, 2011; LaRue, Lenard, Weiss, Bamond, Palmieri & Kelley, 2010),
- *latency-based functional analyses* (LaRue et al., 2010; Thomason-Sassi, Iwata, Neidert & Roscoe, 2011),
- *functional analysis of precursor behavior* (e.g., Smith & Churchill, 2002), and

- *functional analysis of requesting behavior* (LaRue, Sloman, Weiss, Delmolino-Gatley, Hansford, Szalony, Madigan & Lambright, 2011).

Each of these will be described in detail below.

Trial-Based Functional Analyses (TBFA)

TBFA is a brief model of analysis that minimizes the occurrence of problem behavior. TBFA involves briefly exposing the student to conditions similar to those used in a traditional functional analysis (e.g., no attention, restricted access to preferred items, presenting difficult demands) and reinforcing *single instances* of the challenging behavior.

Simply put, you run a functional analysis condition until the first instance of problem behavior or until one minute has elapsed—whichever comes first. You then provide reinforcement (e.g., attention, access to preferred items or activities, or escape) for the second minute. You document whether problem behavior occurred in the first and/or second minute. These procedures are very brief and can be a very useful tool for practitioners and parents with limited resources. Recent research has suggested that TBFAs have reasonably strong correspondence with traditional models of functional analysis (Bloom et al., 2011; LaRue et al., 2010).

When implementing TBFAs, you provide brief exposures to a *test phase* and a *control phase*. These exposures can last about a minute each. The *test phase* looks very similar to that of a regular functional analysis and the *control phase* is the exact opposite, in that the condition is reversed. (A more thorough description of the procedure follows.) Common conditions include attention, tangible, and demand conditions. Alone conditions can also be conducted if automatic reinforcement is suspected.

- *Attention*: In the *test phase* of the attention condition (the first minute), the therapist acts distracted (e.g., gathering materials, writing on a data sheet). This phase lasts for one minute or until the first instance of the target behavior. During the *control phase* of the condition (the second minute), one minute of continuous attention is provided. High levels of problem behavior in the first minute (no attention) relative to the second minute (attention) would suggest a possible attention function.

- *Tangible*: In the *test phase* of the tangible condition (the first minute), access to preferred items or activities is restricted (e.g., the therapist holds the items). This phase lasts for one minute or until the first instance of the target behavior. In the *control phase* of the condition (the second minute), one minute of free access to items/activities is provided. High levels of problem behavior in the first minute (restricted access to items/activities) relative to the second minute (free access) would suggest a possible tangible function.
- *Demand*: In the *test phase* of the demand condition (the first minute), the therapist makes demands on the student (e.g., academics, nonpreferred food or drink) for one minute or until the first instance of the target behavior. In the *control phase* of the demand condition (second minute), one minute of escape from the demands is provided. High levels of problem behavior in the first minute (demands presented) relative to the second minute (no demands) would suggest a possible escape function.
- *Alone/Ignore Condition:* In the alone/ignore condition, the test and control conditions look exactly the same. In the *test phase* (the first minute), the student is left alone in a room (or in a room with the evaluator with no interaction). During the *test phase* (second minute), the same procedure is used. Assuming that the target behavior is automatically reinforced, it should be just as likely to occur in the first minute as it is in the second minute.

To further illustrate the conditions, they are summarized in the table on the next page.

In a TBFA, each test phase (the first minute) is compared to its control phase (the second minute). In general, if the target behavior occurs more frequently in the test phase than in the control phase, it suggests a functional relationship. For example, if a student has attention-maintained problem behavior, it would be more likely to occur when attention is withheld (first minute) than when he has free access to attention (second minute). Similarly, a student with escape-maintained behavior would be more likely to engage in that behavior when demands are presented (first minute) as compared to when no demands are given (second minute).

TBFA Conditions

Conditions	First Minute (Test Phase)	Second Minute (Control Phase)
Social Attention Condition	Therapist pretends to be distracted (e.g., reading)	One minute of attention
Tangible Condition	Access to preferred items/ activities withheld	One minute of access
Demand Condition	Aversive stimuli presented (e.g., difficult academic demands, noise)	One minute of escape
Alone/Ignore Condition	Individual alone in a room (or therapist is present, with no interaction)	Individual alone in a room (or therapist is present, with no interaction)

An example data sheet is provided on page 112. Each row represents a session in each condition type. For example, if the first session you ran was the attention condition (in row 1), no problem behavior was observed in the first or second minutes. The absence of problem behavior is marked as a "–" in the table. If the demand session was run next, the data sheet shows that the target behavior did occur in the first minute and is marked with a "+" sign. (The "time of target" is noted as 13, meaning that 13 seconds elapsed before the student engaged in the behavior.) The behavior did not occur during the second minute when no demands were present (marked with a "–").

The occurrences and nonoccurrences of behaviors are then totaled and converted to a percentage for interpretation. In the example below, in the attention conditions, problem behavior occurred when attention was withheld one out of ten times (10 percent of opportunities) and one out of ten times when the student had free access to attention (10 percent of opportunities). This suggests *no* functional relationship because problem behavior was just as likely to occur regardless of the level of attention. In the demand conditions, problem behavior occurred when demands were presented in eight of ten opportunities (80 percent of the time) and one of ten times during breaks

	Trial-Based Functional Analysis									
	Attention			**Demand**			**Tangible**			**Alone**	
	No Attention	Time of Target	Attention	Demands Present	Time of Target	No Demands	No Access	Time of Target	Access	First Minute	Second Minute
1											
2											
3											
4											
5											
6											
7											
8											
9											
10											
11											
12											
13											
14											
15											

	Trial-Based Functional Analysis									
	Attention			**Demand**			**Tangible**			**Alone**	
	No Attention	Time of Target	Attention	Demands Present	Time of Target	No Demands	No Access	Time of Target	Access	First Minute	Second Minute
1	-	n/a	-	+	13	-	-	n/a	-	-	-
2	-	n/a	-	-	n/a	-	-	n/a	-	-	-
3	-	n/a	-	+	6	-	-	n/a	-	-	-
4	+	47	-	+	27	-	-	n/a	-	-	-
5	-	n/a	-	+	21	-	-	n/a	-	-	-
6	-	n/a	-	+	3	-	-	n/a	+	-	-
7	-	n/a	+	-	n/a	-	-	n/a	-	-	-
8	-	n/a	-	+	40	+	-	n/a	-	-	-
9	-	n/a	-	+	11	-	-	n/a	-	-	-
10	-	n/a	-	+	5	-	-	n/a	-	-	-
11											
12											
13											
14											
15											
	10%		10%	80%		10%	0%		10%	0%	0%

(10 percent of the time). These data suggest that there *is* a functional relationship because problem behavior is much more likely to occur during demands than during breaks.

The percentages obtained from the data sheet can then be graphed for easy interpretation (see figure on the next page).

There are a number of advantages to TBFAs. These procedures are very brief and can be used at naturally occurring times of the day, which can lessen the burden on resources. This is particularly appealing, given that the literature suggests that the results obtained are comparable to those of traditional FAs (Bloom et al., 2011; LaRue et al., 2010). My colleagues and I (RL) (2010) found that sessions could be run during normal classroom activities and reduce total session

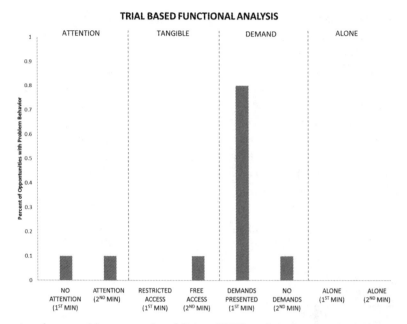

time by over 80 percent. In addition, TBFAs minimize the occurrence of problem behavior, which reduces risk to the student and staff. Research has also shown that treatments based on the results of TBFAs are effective for reducing problem behavior (Bloom, Lambert, Dayton & Samaha, 2013; Lambert, Bloom & Irvin, 2012).

One consideration in using TBFAs is that their effectiveness is linked to the rate of the behavior. TBFAs are only likely to be effective for identifying the function for high frequency behavior (occurring more than once a minute, or within a minute of a certain event such as the presentation of work or the withdrawal of attention). Low frequency behavior is not likely to be captured during a TBFA.

Latency-Based Functional Analyses (LBFA)

LBFAs represent another useful procedural variation for functional analyses. In an LBFA, target behavior is measured in a different way than in other FA models. Rather than counting the number of times a behavior occurs during each condition, you measure the number of seconds from the start of the condition until the *first instance* of the behavior. In other words, you would start a timer at the start of the functional analysis session and stop the timer at the instant the problem behavior occurred. Target behavior that happens very quickly (short latencies) would suggest that it is a high-rate behavior. LBFAs have also been shown to have strong correspondence with traditional models of functional analysis (Thomason-Sassi et al., 2011; LaRue et al., 2010).

These procedures are run in a similar manner as traditional functional analyses. The same five conditions are run using the same antecedent conditions (e.g., withholding attention, presenting demands). The primary difference is that the sessions simply end when the first target behavior occurs. The number of elapsed seconds or minutes is recorded on the data sheet for each condition. An example of an LBFA data sheet is shown below.

LBFA Data Sheet

	Series 1	Series 2	Series 3	Series 4	Series 5
Attention					
Tangible					
Demand					
Alone					
Play					

LBFA Data Sheet

	Series 1	Series 2	Series 3	Series 4	Series 5
Attention	26	102	11	42	36
Tangible	n/a	n/a	n/a	n/a	565
Demand	n/a	356	n/a	n/a	n/a
Alone	552	n/a	498	n/a	n/a
Play	n/a	n/a	n/a	n/a	n/a

The data obtained are then graphed (see below). You will notice that LBFA graphs look similar to traditional FA graphs, but *reversed*. The condition that is likely motivating the behavior has a *lower* number (of seconds) than the control condition. This is because *shorter latencies* are indicative of *greater response strength*. In other words, if the target behavior happens more quickly following the start of a condition, it suggests that it is a high-rate target behavior. In the graph labeled Latency-Based FA below, you will notice that the attention condition consistently has shorter latencies to the first instance of target behavior (e.g., 26 seconds, 102 seconds, etc.), while target behavior is never observed in the control condition. The fact that target behavior occurs primarily in the attention condition and relatively soon after the start of each session strongly suggests that the behavior is maintained by social attention.

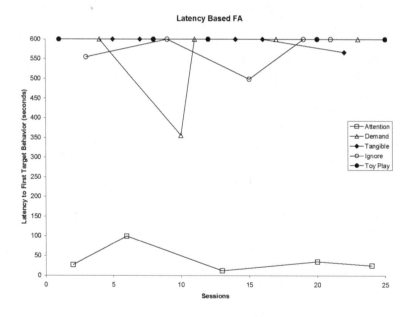

Latency-based models are particularly useful for assessing dangerous behaviors (e.g., severe aggression or self-injury). In an LBFA, the session can end when the behavior begins, which limits exposure to possible injury for the student or evaluator. The fact that LBFAs yield similar results to traditional models of functional analysis, while limiting or blocking problem behavior, makes them a useful tool for behavior assessment (LaRue et al., 2010, Thomason-Sassi, Iwata, Neider & Roscoe, 2011).

Precursor Functional Analyses

In many cases, different *types* of problem behavior may reliably occur together. For example, when having a tantrum, a child may first begin to whine, then scream, then throw items, and then engage in aggression, in that order. If these types of problem behavior occur reliably, it may be possible to conduct a functional analysis for a less severe target behavior that occurs earlier in the chain. For example, for the child described above, it may be possible to conduct the functional analysis for whining/screaming, which may preclude the need to reinforce more dangerous forms of behavior (e.g., aggression).

Prior to conducting a precursor functional analysis, it is important to make sure that the different types of problem behavior do reliably occur together. To accomplish this, you will need to observe whether problem behavior does indeed occur at the same time and in a specific order. The literature suggests that precursor functional analyses can provide similar results to traditional models of assessment (Smith & Churchill, 2002; Borrero & Borrero, 2008; Fritz et al., 2013).

Precursor functional analyses are done using the same general procedures as traditional FA models. The same conditions are run (e.g., attention, demand, tangible) as part of the assessment, but a less severe type of problem behavior that occurs earlier in the response chain is reinforced.

As with some of the other alternative FA models, precursor FAs are particularly helpful when assessing dangerous behaviors (e.g., severe aggression, self-injury). In many cases, severe forms of problem behavior (e.g., aggression and SIB) can be assessed without needing to evoke types that may present the risk for injury.

Functional Analysis of Requesting

Another model that may help circumvent some of the challenges associated with traditional functional analysis involves an analysis of *requesting* behavior. This is because communication difficulties are almost always a contributing factor when people with ASD have behavioral difficulties.

When designing treatments for problem behavior, we usually teach an equivalent response that serves the same purpose that problem behavior does (e.g., Carr & Durand, 1985). This procedure is referred to as *functional communication training*. For example, if a student uses disruptive behavior to get access to attention, we might teach him to request attention appropriately (e.g., raising his hand, touching a "Talk to me" button on a communication device). Similarly, if a student engages in disruptive behavior to escape demands, we might teach him to request help or breaks. When someone has the ability to get access to reinforcement for appropriate communication, it is likely to *increase* communication and *decrease* problem behavior. This is important because it suggests that you can teach different communication responses (e.g., a "break" response, an "attention" response) and conduct a functional analysis of these responses as an alternative to reinforcing problem behavior. In a study in 2011, my colleagues and I (RL) found that *FAs of requesting behavior* corresponded with traditional models of functional analysis for three of four students.

In a functional analysis of requesting, the procedures are very similar to those used with a traditional functional analysis. However, rather than reinforcing challenging behavior, communication responses (e.g., touching a card, signing, or making requests with an augmentative device) are reinforced. Common requesting FA conditions may include:

- *Attention*: You withhold attention during the condition and provide twenty seconds of interaction contingent upon communication (e.g., when the child touches a card). You collect data on how many appropriate requests for attention are made.

- *Tangible*: You restrict access to preferred items/activities and provide twenty seconds of access contingent upon appropriate communication. You collect data on how many appropriate requests for tangibles/activities are made.

- *Demand*: You present continuous demands/aversive stimulation (e.g., academic demands) and provide twenty seconds of escape contingent upon appropriate communication. You collect data on how many appropriate break/help requests are made.

- *Control*: In the control condition, the student has free access to attention and preferred items and activities. No demands are presented. Communication devices should be available during this condition to ensure the individual uses them only when he wants to communicate (rather than just playing with the materials). You collect data on how many appropriate requests are made.

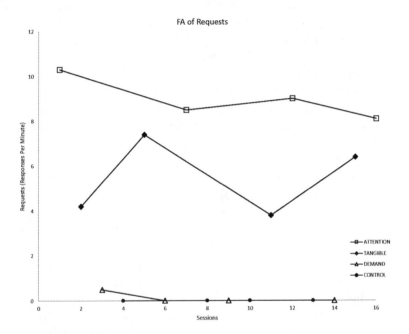

In the graph above you can see that the highest rate of requesting was observed in the attention condition. In addition, you can see that the student also made more requests in the tangible condition than in the control condition. These findings suggest that this student's communication (and therefore problem behavior) is likely to have more than one function.

As with some of the other alternative FA models, requesting FA models are particularly helpful for assessing dangerous behavior (e.g., severe aggression or self-injury). In addition, requesting FAs may also be useful for identifying the function of low-frequency behaviors. These procedures are less intrusive than other models of functional analyses in that problem behavior is not reinforced. However, requesting FAs do not test for multiple types of problem behavior with different functions (e.g., a student who becomes aggressive to escape demands and becomes disruptive to get social attention).

Summary

Functional analysis represents the gold standard for identifying the factors contributing to problem behavior. As a general rule, you should use traditional models of functional analysis whenever possible. There is a great deal of research showing that these methods are effective, and, when used properly, lead to better and less intrusive treatments.

However, there are some circumstances that may require the use of alternative assessment strategies. Lack of resources and ethical concerns about reinforcing problem behavior are common issues that may require the use of alternative strategies to accurately identify the function for challenging behavior. Many professionals struggle with having adequate resources to conduct sound functional analyses. Indeed, traditional models of functional analysis typically require a session room and at least two to three people to be present to run sessions. Trial-based functional analysis (TBFA) may help to alleviate some of these concerns. One of the benefits of TBFA is that students do not necessarily need to be removed from the natural environment. In addition, the brief nature and simple data collection procedures make the TBFA a very useful tool.

Deliberately triggering problem behavior is one of the biggest ethical concerns cited by parents and practitioners. There are several FA models that allow you to gather useful information while keeping the student and those around him safe. The TBFA, LBFA (latency-based functional analysis), precursor FA, and requesting FA all minimize the need to reinforce problem behavior.

While these procedures can be extremely useful tools, there can be drawbacks. The more corners you cut, the more likely it is that you will miss an important relationship. Shorter session lengths may not allow enough time for the learner to develop the motivation to engage in the behavior (e.g., in a trial-based FA, one minute without water might not leave a child thirsty enough to engage in a behavior to get more water). Shorter sessions also may not allow the behavior to occur frequently enough for you to see patterns. When you reinforce lesser levels or alternative forms of target behavior (e.g., a scream that typically occurs before a punch), you may miss important information, particularly if more severe types of problem behavior have different functions.

With the development of functional analysis procedures, treatment for behavior problems among people with ASD and other developmental disabilities has improved dramatically. More than a thousand articles have been published showing the strength of these procedures. Using these methods is clearly the best way to identify the motivation behind an individual's problem behavior. However, there are circumstances in which using traditional procedures may be challenging to implement from an ethical standpoint. Lack of resources, concerns about the safety of the individual and others, and difficulty with identifying the function for low frequency problem behavior are all circumstances that may require practitioners to use variations of traditional functional analysis procedures. TBFAs, LB-FAs, PFAs, and requesting FAs may all be viable strategies that may be useful in these situations.

9 | Putting It All Together
A Summary of the
Assessment Process

R eading through all of the strategies described in the preceding chapters can be overwhelming. You might be thinking, "Where do I begin?" On the next page is a flow chart that lists each of the steps in completing your functional behavior assessment.

After completing all of these steps, you should be able to use your findings to determine the function of the behavior. Following the description of each assessment tool included in this book, you will find directions as to how to use your data to identify the function of the behavior.

On the form that follows the flow chart, list the probable functions of the behavior you have come up with using each assessment tool.

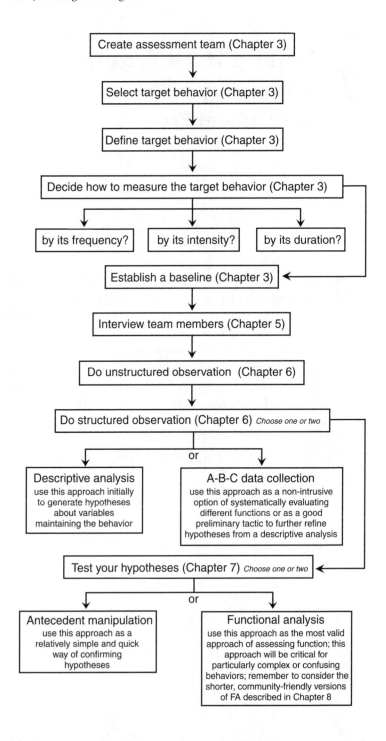

Functional Behavior Assessment Summary Form

Behavior: _____

Definition of Behavior:

_____

_____

_____

_____

Did you suspect any particular function(s) before completing the assessment? If yes, please list:

1. _____

2. _____

3. _____

After reviewing interview data, what are the most likely function(s)?

1. _____

2. _____

3. _____

Based on unstructured observation, what are the most likely function(s)?

1. _____

2. _____

3. _____

Based on structured observation, what are the most likely function(s)?

1. _____

2. _____

3. _____

(Continued on next page.)

Based on hypothesis testing, what are the most likely function(s)?

1. _____

2. _____

3. _____

Any consistent predominant function(s)?

1. _____

2. _____

3. _____

Notes:

If different tools each suggest a different function, does a consistent function emerge within each setting? If so, behavior probably serves a different function in each setting.

If different tools each suggest a different function across all tools and are inconsistent across settings, behavior probably serves multiple functions in each setting.

10 | You Finally Know the Function of the Behavior
Now What?

Congratulations! All your hard work has paid off! You finally know why that seemingly senseless behavior keeps occurring. But, now what? How will this information help you? Detailed instruction regarding setting up a functionally relevant behavior plan is beyond the scope of this book. Nevertheless, because knowing how you will use your assessment information is critical in understanding the assessment process, an introduction to the development of behavior plans is included below. This topic is covered in much greater detail in the companion volume to this book, *Stop That Seemingly Senseless Behavior!*

What Are the Components of an Intervention Plan?

Just as the assessment process grows out of what we know about learning, so does the intervention process. Remember those four keys to learning? 1) The motivating operation (MO), 2) the immediate antecedent, 3) the behavior, and 4) the consequence. It turns out these are the keys to unlearning problem behaviors as well. Therefore, when creating functionally relevant behavior intervention plans, we focus on each of these critical variables. For every behavior plan, each of the four keys to learning must be considered.

Change the MO

First, to change a behavior, you can alter the child's MO for the behavior. If there is no MO for the behavior in place, it will not occur.

One way to alter the MO for a given behavior is to enrich the person's environment in such a way that the behavior will never be evoked. For example, if the function of a child's problem behavior is to obtain attention, then give the child more attention throughout the day. Specifically, if you know that he usually can go about ten minutes without attention before exhibiting the problem behavior, be sure to provide attention at least every eight minutes. Over time, you can introduce other teaching strategies to help him tolerate longer and longer periods of low attention. By controlling the establishing operation in this way, you can ensure that the target behavior never occurs. This will prevent the child from practicing the behavior, which prevents him from being reinforced for the behavior, which ultimately helps make the behavior obsolete.

Some points of intervention that fall under this approach include:

1. addressing any issues related to physiological problems (e.g., a child who uses problem behaviors to escape a task because he is too sleepy to work, or a child whose allergies make him too uncomfortable to concentrate on a social interaction);

2. setting-related variables (e.g., a child who uses a behavior to escape from an environment that is too brightly lit, or an adolescent who engages in self-talk whenever things are too quiet); or

3. contextual variables (e.g., a child who exhibits behavior problems in crowds, or an adult who has behavior problems only when she is assigned housekeeping duties at the hotel where she works).

In many cases, addressing the behavior solely by controlling the person's MO will eliminate a problem behavior. The downside of using this approach in isolation is that the individual does not learn how to manage that MO if it arises in some less-controlled setting. Because it is often impossible to prevent a specific MO from ever being in effect, it is almost guaranteed that the person will need to learn how to manage that MO effectively.

Change the Antecedents

Next, an intervention focuses on immediate antecedents. If you have identified consistent immediate antecedents for a behavior through your assessment, you will want to examine these and attempt to change them where possible. Sometimes changing a seemingly minor cue will completely alter a behavior. For example, if a child launches into challenging behaviors whenever she sees her work desk, allowing her to work on the floor instead can help to eliminate the behavior. Similarly, if a child has a history of resisting bedtime, she may be more cooperative if you call it "rest time."

Of course, you cannot always rely on this approach because antecedents that trigger problem behaviors cannot always be eliminated. When you are potty training a child, for example, the toilet will always be involved. If sirens set off a behavior, you cannot shield the student from sirens forever. Furthermore, changing antecedents may not be an option for automatic reinforcement behaviors, as the antecedent may sometimes occur inside of the person.

Change the Behavior

The third key component in the learning equation is the behavior itself. In your intervention plan, you will not only attempt to rid the individual of the problem behavior, but you will also ensure that he acquires a new behavior to get his needs met.

This step is probably the most critical in developing a successful plan. You will want to choose a replacement behavior that is simple for the individual to acquire and will lead to reinforcement for him. Recall from our overview of learning theory that a more efficient behavior will always replace a less efficient behavior. Therefore, replacement behaviors must be carefully selected to compete with problem behaviors. You need to find a behavior that will allow the person to get what he wants more quickly and consistently than the problem behavior does. For example, if Kayla vomits after taking one bite of food as a way to avoid eating certain meals, we can teach her to ask for something different. If Joey hits the teacher when the work is too boring, we can teach him to ask for different work.

Similarly, if Anthony is banging his head as a means of requesting his favorite beads, then you might teach him to hand over a picture card to request the beads. This would be an effective replacement behavior only if the card is clearly identifiable, easily accessible, and entails minimal challenge for Anthony. In short, the picture exchange will replace the head banging if it is an easier way to obtain the same result.

In order to teach Anthony to request the beads using the picture exchange, you might consider hanging a photo of the beads in every room. Starting in one room with the beads next to you but out of his reach, you might prompt Anthony to take the card and hand it to you. Then, you'd say something like "Oh, you want the beads; great telling me you want the beads," as you hand him the beads. After Anthony had two or three minutes with the beads, you would remove the beads, again placing them within his sight but out of his reach. The entire process would then be repeated.

After a few cycles fully prompting Anthony, you might gradually fade back your prompts and see if he can request the beads independently in this scenario. As he gains proficiency at this, you would gradually increase the demand by increasing Anthony's distance from the beads, and gradually putting them out of sight. Once Anthony was proficient at requesting the beads with the photo when he was in the room with them, you would have him practice in other rooms. At that point, Anthony should start to request the beads independently.

In some cases, it might take an individual quite a while to learn a replacement skill, but teaching the replacement skill should nevertheless be part of the intervention, as this will be critical in maintaining long-term success.

Change the Consequences

The final component in the learning equation is the consequence. When intervening on a problem behavior, you will aim to reverse the consequence that the individual has learned to expect. Continuing our example above, Anthony must no longer get the beads as a consequence for head banging. Instead, Anthony should receive beads immediately for using his picture exchange skills.

Sometimes it will not be possible to immediately reverse the consequence of a problem behavior. This is more likely to be the case if self-injurious or otherwise dangerous behavior is involved. Perhaps Anthony's family needs to give Anthony the beads to get him to stop banging his head. In cases like this, be sure that the consequence for the replacement behavior far surpasses the consequence for the challenging behavior in terms of quality and quantity. This contrast will lead to the challenging behavior disappearing. Based on this principle, Anthony's family might give Anthony two or three of the least interesting beads if he bangs his head, but twenty or thirty of his favorite beads if he requests beads with his picture card.

When a child is more verbal or has stronger cognitive skills, it might be helpful to let him know about the change in rules and consequences. For example, recall the obsession that Darra, from the introduction, has with the band One-D. Darra's mother might say something to her like, "Darra, I know you love to talk about One-D, but other people get tired of hearing about them all day. Other kids would probably be more interested in being your friend if you sometimes talked about things *they* wanted to talk about. I'm afraid I'm going to have to ignore you if you talk about One-D, but I will be happy to talk with you about anything else...."

As with any behavioral intervention, informing someone of the new rules means nothing if you don't stick to what you say. Therefore, before reversing any contingency, be sure to choose an approach that you, and everyone else responsible for working with your child or student, can stick to. For example, if Darra's mother knows that Darra's teacher gets so irritated by the One-D talk that she will not be able to ignore it, then another approach that everyone can consistently use must be selected.

Choosing Strategies to Match the Function of the Behavior

The guidelines described above highlight the various components of an intervention. Next, you will learn some basic steps to developing each of these components for a specific behavior based on your functional behavior assessment results. To accomplish this, you need to answer further assessment questions. The answers to these questions will help pinpoint specific strategies. Further assessment questions for the four basic functions of behavior are included below.

For Attention-Maintained Behaviors

What is the quality of attention that the person with the problem behavior is seeking?

- Will any attention do?

- Is it peer attention?
- Is it adult attention?
- Is it undivided attention?
- Is it high intensity attention?
- Is it physical attention?
- Is it a certain person's attention?
- How long can the individual go between instances of this type of attention without exhibiting the problem behavior?

Use the answers to these questions to guide your intervention. For example, if your child uses his problem behavior to get high intensity attention, you should give him that attention on a rich schedule regardless of his behavior. Additionally, you should praise him in an animated and high intensity fashion when you see him using appropriate methods of obtaining attention. Furthermore, you might teach him to request a game that results in high intensity attention (e.g., tickle tag) and reinforce these requests consistently at first. Finally, make sure that problem behaviors do not result in your child obtaining the desired attention.

Although you cannot consistently control all of the variables—such as peer attention—you will be surprised at how much you can actually accomplish by putting forth your best effort. For example, imagine that a child is using a problem behavior (e.g., wisecracks) to get his classmates' attention. Setting up class-wide contingencies (such as establishing a rule that anyone who laughs at another student's wisecracks during class gets five extra minutes of homework) can cut peer attention enough to make the intervention effective.

For Escape-Maintained Behaviors

- What is the individual with autism escaping?
- Is the demand too challenging?
- Is the demand too boring?
- Is the demand centered around nonpreferred materials?
- Is the demand associated with a certain type of stimulation?
- Is the demand social?
- Is the demand specific to a certain person?
- Does the demand go on for too long?

Again, you will create your intervention around the answers to these questions. For example, you might determine that a behavior occurs because your child or student finds a task too boring. If so, you might make the task a bit harder, use more preferred materials, and tackle goals in a more preferred format (e.g., playing a game rather than completing a worksheet). You might teach your child to appropriately request new tasks and consistently reinforce appropriate requests at first. Problem behaviors should not result in escaping the demand.

Sometimes behaviors are reinforced when you remove a stimulus or a person that you do not want to remove. For example, your child might exhibit a problem behavior to escape or avoid taking a bath. However, you cannot just teach your child to request to skip his bath, as he needs to be clean. In this instance, you might try to isolate the variable that your child most dislikes. For example, does he especially dislike the water running in his face during shampooing? Then, having him wear a visor might solve the problem. Does he dislike the washcloth? Try using a scrubbing puff.

Similarly, children sometimes use problem behaviors to avoid contact with certain people, such as siblings or specific instructors. Nevertheless, escaping these people permanently is not an option. For this situation, use the same approach described in our bath example, above. Try to identify what it is about the person that the child finds aversive. Is the sibling's presence associated with less attention from Mom? Then perhaps you should really be intervening based on divided attention. Is the sibling associated with any positive activities? If not, it may help to pair the brother or sister with the child's favorite treats and activities. Sometimes people with ASD avoid certain individuals due to some idiosyncratic variable like the smell of their perfume or the sound of their squeaky sneakers. Once identified, these variables are simple to address.

For Behaviors Maintained by Access to Objects and Activities

- What activities or objects does the individual get from the behavior?
- Does the behavior occur when it's time to give up access?
- Does the behavior occur when he needs to wait for access?
- Does the behavior occur when he needs to share?
- Does the behavior occur when he needs to take turns?

As with the behavior plan ideas listed above, you will create your intervention around the answers to these questions. For example, a behavior that occurs when a child needs to take turns might be addressed by giving him more access to the item throughout the day, offering warnings of how much time is left before he needs to give up his turn, teaching him to request a little more time and initially reinforcing this request, providing a powerful reinforcer for sharing, and requiring him to share even if he exhibits the problem behavior.

For Behaviors Maintained by Automatic Reinforcement

- What exactly is the sensation that the individual is obtaining with the problem behavior?
- Is the behavior related to a medical problem (e.g., head banging during an ear infection)?

Automatic reinforcement behaviors are the trickiest to tackle. First of all, identifying the exact sensation that the child is obtaining from the behavior may pose a challenge. If possible, try the behavior yourself to see what sensations you experience. Some common sensations associated with automatic behaviors include vestibular stimulation (e.g., from rocking or spinning), dizziness, visual input (e.g., from watching hand-flapping or running back and forth by a fence), feeling pleasurable textures (e.g., from rubbing stockings or handling soft materials), a meditative state (e.g., from humming or rocking), or reliving pleasurable experiences (e.g., from self-talk or singing).

People often wonder what type of desirable feedback could possibly come from self-injury. One plausible theory suggests that endorphins, chemicals associated with peaceful and happy feelings that are naturally released in the brain in response to an injury, are somehow more acutely active for these individuals than for the average person. If that were indeed the case, then it would make sense that self-injury would lead to a sense of "rush."

If you cannot try the behavior yourself, as in the case of self-injurious or dangerous behaviors, you will have to use trial and error to try to determine what the person gets out of the behavior. Obviously, if the behavior is related to a medical problem, treat the medical problem.

Once you have an idea of the sensation the individual is getting from his behavior, try to identify a more appropriate source of the same stimulation for him. Some common examples might involve introducing a rocking chair for someone who rocks, a portable mp3 player for someone who sings to himself, a fan for someone who flaps his hands, or gloves for someone who wraps his own hands up with fabric.

You can also try to link the behavior to a certain setting. For example, you might try to establish a "talking chair," a chair that serves as the only place a child is allowed to engage in self-talk. Then, any time you observe your child talking to himself, you would guide him to that chair. This approach can also work for people who need others around to satisfy their motivation. For example, if Darra wanted to talk to someone about One-D, you could designate one specific person who will listen to the talk in one specific place. For example, Darra could talk to her mom in her room. If she started to talk about One-D at school, her teachers could interrupt and tell her that discussing One-D is something special between her and her mother. At home, Darra could be taught to say to her mother, "Can we go to my room and talk about One-D?" A timer could then be set and she could have her need met without stigmatizing herself. As long as One-D talk is not responded to or accepted in other environments or with other people, Darra would quickly learn to make this request.

In our everyday lives, we learn contingencies such as this all the time. For example, we all have friends who gossip and friends who don't. We have friends to whom we admit that we ate an entire box of cookies, and friends who would be disgusted by our confession. We quickly learn these contingencies and get our reinforcement where we can.

In general, effective intervention for automatic reinforcement behaviors focuses on finding a harmless way to get the child the stimulation that he is seeking. Like any other attempts to stop a behavior without teaching new skills, they will be fruitless if the child does not have another way to get his needs met.

One of the easiest strategies for targeting automatic reinforcement behaviors is to enrich the environment with preferred objects, people, and activities. Often when children with ASD are provided with sufficient external stimulation, they no longer feel the need to provide their own stimulation.

Matching Treatment to Function

	Maintained by Social Attention	Maintained by Access to Tangibles	Maintained by Escape from Demands	Maintained by Automatic Reinforcement
Antecedent-Based Strategies	Provide noncontingent attention Increase opportunities for appropriate social interaction	Provide noncontingent access to preferred items Teach them to request items appropriately	Provide frequent breaks Take a step back and make sure they have the prerequisite skills	Allow the behavior at certain times of the day (assuming it is not dangerous) Introduce items that compete with the behavior
Consequence-Based Strategies	Reinforce appropriate requests for attention (FCT) Extinction (no attention following problem behavior)	Reinforce appropriate requests for preferred items (FCT) Extinction (no access to items following problem behavior)	Reinforce appropriate requests for escape/breaks (FCT) Escape extinction (no breaks provided following problem behavior)	Reinforce appropriate requests to engage in the behavior (FCT) Differential reinforcement (e.g., DRO, DRI)
Contraindicated Strategies	Reprimands	"Giving in" (allowing access to tangibles)	Time-out	Medication only

Special Circumstances and Troubleshooting

For assessing all but the most challenging behaviors in children and adults with autism spectrum disorders, the information and guidelines presented up until this point will be sufficient to lead to effective intervention. Nevertheless, there are some situations that require special attention for various reasons. For example, there are some special considerations to keep in mind when doing functional behavior assessments of adolescents or adults, or when assessing dangerous but infrequent behaviors. To meet these challenges, you'll need to become a functional behavior assessment "specialist." Ideas for working with these special populations and situations, as well as for troubleshooting when behavioral functions and interventions are not clear, are included below.

Adolescents and Adults

Although you will use the same general strategies for completing functional behavior assessments with adolescents and adults that you use with children, there are some special considerations to keep in mind.

Safety Issues

First and foremost, keep the individual's size in mind. Because adolescents and adults are bigger and stronger than younger children, you will need to exercise particular caution with regard to escalation of behaviors. As you would when completing an assessment with a child, be sure to stop any assessment that is placing someone in danger and switch to crisis management mode immediately. "Crisis management" mode implies that a long-term treatment for a behavior is no longer the priority. Instead, preserving everyone's safety becomes an immediate priority. You may need to actually reinforce a challenging behavior (assuming that you know what will do so) in order to make it end. While this is counterintuitive regarding the treatment of challenging behaviors, it is the logical choice in the realm of common sense—safety first! You can follow up with a thorough assessment and intervention later.

Some of the assessment strategies described actually evoke the problem behavior, and may even evoke a more intense form of the behavior. Do not use these approaches when assessing aggressive, self-injurious, or destructive behaviors without the supervision of an experienced behavior analyst trained in crisis management procedures. If such supervision is not available, consider inpatient placement at a facility where the function of the person's behavior can be identified while preserving everyone's safety. Contact your school district or a local board certified behavior analyst (see www.BACB.com) for assistance in finding an inpatient placement near you.

As a final safety note, when choosing interventions for adolescents and adults with potentially dangerous behaviors, consider relying on interventions based on changing EOs and immediate antecedents whenever possible. This will preserve safety for everyone, as it will prevent the behavior from occurring at all, rather than requiring you to respond to it.

Some clients I have worked with question whether or not it is acceptable to keep these proactive interventions in place permanently to prevent the problem behavior. They are concerned that the individual is not functioning independently if he or she always needs these supports. For example, consider a young man with an ASD and intellectual disability who requires brief social attention such as a smile and pat on the back every fifteen minutes in order to prevent severe, destructive behaviors. Would I recommend that this intervention remain in place permanently? I absolutely would. Unless it would cause significant hardship to those around the individual, leaving an intervention in place permanently to avoid a serious behavior problem would be worth it.

Just as some individuals have disabilities that require wheelchairs or the use of braille, some individuals have disabilities that require other forms of support. As long as it is feasible to provide what is needed, I would not be concerned about whether or not a person "should" need a support that prevents significant problem behaviors. Teaching the person to do without that support may be possible, but why not improve the quality of her life and skip all of the risk involved in trying to teach her to do without it at the same time?

Allowing Enough Time to Learn a New Behavior

Another consideration when addressing problem behaviors in adolescents and adults is the length of time they have engaged in the problem behavior. Depending on the particular behavior, the individual may have been effectively practicing a certain problematic response for a very long time. The longer a behavior has been practiced, the longer it will take to be replaced. For example, have you ever written the previous year on a check just after New Year's? It takes a while to unlearn the well-practiced response of writing the previous year. Have you ever moved to a new home and accidentally written your old return address on an envelope? You had practiced writing the previous address for a long time and it will take longer to stop that practice than it would to stop writing an address you've written once or twice. When a behavior has persisted a long time, it should be easier to evoke during the assessment process but take longer to successfully address during intervention.

On the flip side, do not assume that because adolescents and adults are older, they have had opportunities to learn appropriate behaviors. When older adults with autism spectrum disorders were children, teaching strategies were not as sophisticated as they are today. Every year, the field progresses and existing teaching practices may be improved. When completing a functional behavior assessment for an adolescent or adult, pay particularly close attention to assessing communication skills as well as to identifying what activities the person can perform independently. Also take note of how much access she has to her preferences. Especially if someone has a more limited educational history, you may find that others know very little about her preferences. Consequently, her life is probably desperately in need of enrichment.

Part of an assessment for someone in this situation might involve comparing the strength of the behavior under enriched versus impoverished environments. For example, imagine an adult who has lived in an institutional setting for most of her life who is now moving into a group home. This individual may at first exhibit many significant behavior problems. As group home staff become more familiar with her, they may discover that she likes to take walks, or that she enjoys watching *Wheel of Fortune*. They may also discover that her favorite food is waffles and her favorite drink is tea. They may teach her some requesting skills to obtain preferred items and activities. Furthermore, she might receive much more attention than she did in her institutional placement. In this new, enriched environment, it would be very surprising if her behavior problems did not decrease. As more of her needs are met, and she has more skills to get her needs met, there would be less and less reason for her to exhibit a challenging behavior.

Choosing the Right Setting for an Assessment

Finally, when working with adolescents and adults, you may need to assess behaviors that occur outside the home or school. For example, you may be faced with assessing a problem behavior that occurs on a jobsite. Evoking the behavior in that setting may be frightening and confusing to customers or other workers who might be present. In this case, you might have to replicate the conditions on the jobsite as best as possible in a more controlled setting, such as the individual's classroom or home. This might involve role playing by members of the assessment team, or it might involve inviting people from the jobsite to come to the classroom or home.

For individuals who live in supervised settings such as group homes, there may be privacy concerns when completing an assessment. For example, other clients should not have access to information about one particular client's problem behavior or assessment conditions. Finding a place to conduct the assessment without the other residents' awareness might pose a challenge.

A particularly challenging situation could arise if an adult with ASD has a problem behavior that disturbs a roommate or that evokes problem behaviors from a housemate. To the best of your ability, you must keep the housemate safe and communicate to him or her that the behavior is being addressed, without sharing any more information than is necessary.

Keep these variables in mind when conducting your assessment. Be sure to speak to relevant staff to gather necessary information.

Rare, but Dangerous, Behaviors

Some problem behaviors occur very infrequently, but neverthe-less pose significant risks to people and property. The severity of these behaviors demands intervention, yet their low rate of occurrence makes that intervention difficult. Because the behavior occurs rarely, it can be difficult or impossible to observe naturally occurring patterns in the behavior or to contrive situations to evoke the behavior. For instance, one adolescent with whom I (BG) worked had such severe aggressive behavior and tantrums on the bus ride home from school that the driver feared for his own safety and had to pull over and call school personnel to come and pick up the student. This happened twice during the entire school year. As you might imagine, it was very hard to gather information as to the function of the behavior since so little observational data was available.

For these types of behaviors, special assessment procedures are required. As with other behaviors, you will still assemble an interven-tion team, define the behavior, and determine how to measure it if it does occur. However, you may not be able to establish a baseline as you would with other behaviors because too much time might pass between occurrences for a pattern to be established. Instead, you will have to rely heavily on interviewing people familiar with the individual and the behavior to gather as much information about patterns of the behavior as possible. Also, ask those who have observed the behavior to complete A-B-C data sheets from memory.

Although relying on other people's recall of events is not ideal, if you collect consistent responses from multiple observers, it can support resulting hypotheses. Based on these information gathering approaches, you are poised to develop some ideas about the possible function of the behavior, institute an interim intervention, and gather more information about the behavior if it does recur.

Finally, everyone who might be responsible for the individual at any given time must be provided with training in crisis management strategies to preserve everyone's safety. For the student who exhibited dangerous behaviors on the bus, interviews with those close to him suggested that he was most likely to engage in problem behavior when he was receiving little attention and had nothing else to do. Conse-quently, he was provided with a bag of preferred snacks and activities for the bus ride, and the driver was trained to interact with him briefly every few minutes. This approach was effective in preventing further occurrences of his aggressive behavior.

Troubleshooting

There are two broad types of trouble spots that arise when using functional behavior assessment with people with autism spectrum disorders. Problems arise when:

1. The assessment results are highly inconsistent, making it difficult to determine the function of the behavior. Or:
2. You think you have determined the function of the behavior, but an intervention designed around that function does not work.

When Assessment Results Are Inconsistent

The first possible stumbling block is posed by highly inconsistent assessment results. In this scenario, any or all of the following may be true:

- Each person interviewed by the team coordinator offers different information and different opinions about why the behavior is occurring.
- No two reporters agree on the actual antecedents and consequences of the behavior.
- Observational data yields inconsistent results.

Sometimes assessment results are inconsistent because the behavior is so unclear. Other times this might occur when different observers and reporters have preconceived notions about the behavior that they are seeking to affirm. In other circumstances, conflicting reports may result because reporters feel pressured to paint a certain picture. For example, teaching staff may not want to suggest that the behavior occurs because their student's work is too uninteresting. Face these problems head on when you suspect them and reassure staff that your assessment is not an evaluation of their work.

Nevertheless, despite your best efforts, you might remain stumped. Try your best to assess just one variable at a time and be creative and observant in developing your hypotheses.

If you remain stumped after your best efforts, try an intervention that addresses attention, escape from demands, and access to preferred items. For example, you might 1) teach a child appropriate requests for all three potential reinforcers, 2) do your best not to respond at all to the challenging behavior when it occurs, and 3) enrich the child's environment with attention, preferred items and activities, and interesting, functional tasks. This will likely lead to decreases in the problem behavior, although you may never find out why.

When an Intervention Doesn't Work

A second stumbling block that may occur relates to the intervention. You have completed a thorough functional behavior assessment and you are sure that you have identified the function of the behavior. You develop an intervention based on these findings and—it doesn't work. First, there are various aspects of the intervention to evaluate:

- Does it actually match the function identified?
- Does it address EOs, antecedents, replacement behaviors, and consequences?
- Is it being implemented according to plan? By everyone who encounters the behavior?

If the answer to all of these questions is yes, you may need to complete a brief reassessment of the behavior. It is possible for the function of a behavior to change. For example, one child I (BG) worked with used to spit during teaching sessions because he enjoyed watching the spit fly through the air and land on something. Part of the intervention that was developed for this behavior involved having him wipe up the spit immediately. Because he cleaned up the spit during teaching sessions, it often delayed his work so that he would get less work done each day. This student quickly learned to use the spitting behavior to meet a second function: escaping class work. A new plan to address this escape behavior in addition to automatic reinforcement needed to be developed. This plan involved reworking the student's tasks to make them more appropriate and interesting, teaching him an appropriate way to request a break, ignoring the spitting in the classroom, and allowing him to request to spit into the toilet.

If you need to reassess a behavior after a plan has been developed, a briefer assessment may suffice. After all, the behavior will already have been defined and a measurement system will already have been developed. Consider relying on just a couple of interviews as well as some structured observation. This abbreviated approach, coupled with careful thinking about how the plan changed the environment for the child, may lead to a successful intervention.

Some behaviors may take a little longer to change. Recall that the longer a behavior is in someone's repertoire, the longer it will take to change. These behaviors will eventually be replaced as the person practices replacement behaviors and receives reinforcement for them. Returning to our example about writing the correct year on checks, we all eventually do learn to write the correct year. Similarly, if you drive "on autopilot" and keep finding yourself heading to your old home after you have moved, you will eventually start driving to your new home. Challenging behaviors are no different; these too will eventually be replaced.

Some behaviors based on avoidance may be particularly difficult to change. Each time the person avoids the feared scenario, her escape behavior grows stronger. Imagine Lily, a three-year-old girl who develops a painful urinary tract infection and then refuses to urinate. She has to be taken to the hospital and catheterized and after this harrowing experience still refuses to urinate. Each time she avoids urination and her perception of the associated pain, her avoidance behaviors are strengthened. Because she experienced the pain associated with urination on an intermittent schedule, urinating once or twice without pain does not convince her that it will be painless the next time.

For avoidance behaviors of this nature, you need to consider a number of strategies. First, if possible, teach the person how to respond if the feared event does occur. For instance, Lily could be reminded that she can stop urination in midstream, and any pain will stop instantly. Also consider using strong motivators to persuade the individual to complete the behavior. For Lily, using a star chart that led to a reward of ice cream (a highly preferred consequence) actually worked in getting her to resume urination. Finally, consider changing the environment where the avoided activity or item is encountered. For Lily, we might have tried a different bathroom than she usually uses, or we could have added a potty seat on top of the toilet, redecorated the bathroom with new character towels and pictures, or let her decorate the lid of the toilet with removable stickers.

Success Stories

Aaron

Aaron was a fifteen-year-old boy with ASD. Aaron's favorite way to interact with people was to poke, swat, and tickle them. Aaron poked his peers, his teachers, his parents, his siblings, and familiar adults who came over to the house. Because Aaron was in an inclusive educational setting, this behavior was extremely stigmatizing for him. While he was participating in an inclusive camp setting, Aaron had unfortunately been severely teased by the boys in his group as a result of the poking. Although he was devastated by their treatment of him, he persisted in poking.

Interview and observation left some confusion about whether the behavior was maintained by attention or based on automatic reinforcement. Through antecedent manipulations, it was determined that the behavior primarily served an automatic reinforcement function, although some team members argued vehemently that attention-seeking played a role. The team members agreed that the automatic reinforcement function would be treated first, so they could see how much of the behavior was left and in which settings it occurred.

Treatment involved teaching Aaron to request "tickle time" and also offering it to him at least once each day. "Tickle time" initially took place in the playroom with Aaron's mother only, but was later transferred to Aaron's one-to-one instructor when the level of touch became uncomfortable for Aaron's mother. Whenever Aaron initiated poking outside of "tickle time," he was reminded that there was a specific time and place where that occurred. During "tickle time," Aaron and his instructor poked, swatted, and tickled intensely, laughed, and thoroughly enjoyed themselves. By the end of the school year, Aaron's poking behavior had disappeared entirely from all settings except during the designated tickle time. In fact, there never was a need to address any supposed attention issues related to the behavior.

Sophie

Sophie was a five-year-old girl who loved other children but lacked the social skills to initiate interactions with them effectively. In a group, Sophie used to immediately run up to other children and provoke them while laughing and smiling. She might push them, steal their toys, or pull their hair. Information obtained through interview and structured observation strongly supported that Sophie used these behaviors in order to obtain attention from peers. It was decided that there was enough confidence based on these two assessment techniques that no further assessment was needed.

In order to treat Sophie's rough and tumble initiation strategy, she was provided with scripted language to use with peers just prior to each play date or group socialization activity. In particular, three comments or questions that Sophie could use with peers were modeled for her each time. Additionally, Sophie was promised ten minutes of extra playtime for keeping her hands to herself throughout the interaction. Data were collected on Sophie's physical behaviors as well as whether or not she used one of the modeled phrases. Almost immediately, Sophie replaced her more aggressive methods with these newly modeled phrases. After two months, Sophie began generalizing previously modeled phrases and coming up with original conversation openers of her own. Finally, the modeling was dropped, and Sophie continued to keep her hands off the other children. The naturally occurring reinforcement from peers for her more appropriate initiations was all the motivation that Sophie needed to maintain her newly acquired skills.

Ramone

Ramone was an eighteen-year-old man with autism who was admitted to a day program for individuals with severe behaviors. Ramone frequently punched staff members, other clients, and visitors to the program. Interview and observation had revealed that Ramone was likely to punch others when there were crowds, work tasks for him to complete, and social demands, as well as when Ramone wanted food or drinks. No specific predominant function had been identified for his behavior. Furthermore, antecedent manipulations did not implicate one function as stronger than the others.

Because his behaviors were so severe, Ramone had historically been allowed to do whatever he liked, unfettered by demands or restrictions. In part because prior staff had hesitated to place educational demands upon him, Ramone had no communication system other than grunting and limited gesturing.

As a first step, Ramone's environment was enriched through a "pairing" procedure in which attempts were made to associate staff and *the new setting with preferred items and activities. Ramone was given plenty of free access to preferred items and activities. Next, Ramone was taught a few basic communicative signs. In particular, he was taught to request certain food items, to request some space, to request a break, and to request attention. Finally, whenever he punched, he continued to be restrained, as staff feared for their safety. These simple changes led to a huge decrease in Ramone's aggressive behavior. This improvement was maintained over time and carried over into Ramone's home. Eventually, Ramone's aggression diminished so much that he was able to obtain supervised employment and work outside of the school.*

References

Bloom, S. E., Iwata B. A., Fritz J. N., Roscoe E. M., & Carreau A. B. (2011). Classroom application of a trial-based functional analysis. *Journal of Applied Behavior Analysis, 44,* 19–31.

Bloom S. E., Lambert, J. M., Dayton, E., & Samaha, A. L. (2013). Teacher-conducted trial-based functional analyses as the basis for intervention. *Journal of Applied Behavior Analysis, 46 (1),* 208–18.

Borrero, C. S. W., & Borrero, J.C. (2008). Descriptive and experimental analyses of potential precursors to problem behavior. *Journal of Applied Behavior Analysis, 41 (1),* 83–96.

Carr, E. G., & Durand, V. M. (1985). Reducing behavior problems through functional communication training. *Journal of Applied Behavior Analysis, 18,* 111–26.

Catania, A. C. (1998). *Learning.* Upper Saddle River, NJ: Simon & Schuster.

Crone, D. A., Hawken, L. S., & Bergstrom, M. K. (2007). A demonstration of training, implementing, and using functional behavioral assessment in 10 elementary and middle school settings. *Journal of Positive Behavior Interventions, 9 (1),* 15–29.

Frea, W. D., & Hughes, C. (1997). Functional analysis and treatment of social-communicative behavior of adolescents with developmental disabilities. *Journal of Applied Behavior Analysis, 30,* 701–704.

Fritz, J. N., Iwata, B. A., Hammond, J. L., & Bloom, S. E. (2013). Experimental analysis of precursors to severe problem behavior. *Journal of Applied Behavior Analysis, 46,* 101–129.

Iwata, B. A., Pace, G. M., Dorsey, M. F., Zarcone, J. R., Vollmer, T. R., Smith, R. G., Rodgers, T. A., Lerman, D. C., Shore, B. A., Mazaleski, J. L., Goh, H.-L., Cowdery, G. E., Kalsher, M. J., McCosh, K. C., & Willis, K. D. (1994). The functions of self-injurious behavior: An experimental-epidemiological analysis. *Journal of Applied Behavior Analysis, 27,* 215–40.

Iwata, B. A., Dorsey, M. F., Slifer, K. J., Bauman, K. E., & Richman, G. S. (1982). Toward a functional analysis of self-injury. *Analysis and Intervention in Developmental Disabilities, 2,* 3–20.

Kern, L., Dunlap, G., Clarke, S., & Childs, K. (1994). Student-assisted functional assessment interview. *Diagnostique,19 (2–3),* 29–39.

Kwak, M. M., Ervin, R. A., Anderson, M. Z., & Austin, J. (2004). Agreement of function across methods used in school-based functional assessment with preadolescent and adolescent students. *Behavior Modification, 28 (3),* 375-401.

Lambert, J. M., Bloom, S. E., & Irvin, J. (2012). Trial-based functional analysis and functional communication training in an early childhood setting. *Journal of Applied Behavior Analysis, 45(3),* 579–84.

Laraway, S., Snycerski, S., Michael, J., & Poling, A. (2003). Motivating operations and some terms to describe them: Some further refinements. *Journal of Applied Behavior Analysis, 36 (3)* 407–14.

LaRue, R. H., Lenard, K., Weiss, M. J., Bamond, M., Palmieri, M., & Kelley, M. E. (2010). Comparison of traditional and trial-based methodologies for conducting functional analyses. *Research in Developmental Disabilities, 31,* 480–87.

LaRue, R. H., Sloman, K., Weiss, M. J., Delmolino-Gatley, L., Hansford, A., Szalony, J., Madigan, R., & Lambright, N. (2011). Correspondence between traditional models of functional analysis and a functional analysis of manding behavior. *Research in Developmental Disabilities, 32,* 2449–57.

Love, J.R., Carr, J. E., & Leblanc, L. (2009). Functional assessment of problem behavior in children with autism spectrum disorders: A summary of 32 outpatient cases. *Journal of Autism and Developmental Disorders, 39,* 363–72.

McLaren, E. M., & Nelson, C. M. (2009). Using functional behavior assessment to develop behavior interventions for children in head start. *Journal of Positive Behavior Interventions, 11,* 3–21

Ratner, S. C. (1970). Habituation: Research and theory. In J. H. Reynierse (Ed.), *Current Issues in Animal Learning* (pp. 55–84). Lincoln, NE: University of Nebraska Press.

Reed, H., Thomas, E., Sprague, J. R., & Horner, R. H. (1997). The student guided functional assessment interview: An analysis of student and teacher agreement. *Journal of Behavioral Education, 7 (1),* 33–49.

Repp, A. C., Felce, D., & Barton, L. E. (1988). Basing the treatment of stereotypic and self-injurious behaviors on hypotheses of their causes. *Journal of Applied Behavior Analysis, 21,* 281–89.

Skinner, B. F. (1953). *Science and Human Behavior.* New York, NY: Macmillan.

Skinner, B. F. (1984). The operational analysis of psychological terms. *Behavioral and Brain Sciences, 7,* 547–82.

Smith, R. G., & Churchill, R. M. (2002). Identification of environmental determinants of behavior disorders through functional analysis of precursor behaviors. *Journal of Applied Behavior Analysis, 35,* 125–36.

Thomason-Sassi, J. L., Iwata, B. A., & Fritz, J. N. (2013). Therapist and setting influences on functional analysis outcomes. *Journal of Applied Behavior Analysis, 46,* 79–87.

Touchette P. E., MacDonald R. F., & Langer S. N. (1985). A scatter plot for identifying stimulus control of problem behavior. *Journal of Applied Behavior Analysis, 18 (4),* 343–51.

Vollmer, T. R., & Iwata, B. A. (1991). Establishing operations and reinforcement effects. *Journal of Applied Behavior Analysis, 24,* 279–91.

Wallace, M. D., & Iwata, B. A. (1999). Effects of session duration on functional analysis outcomes. *Journal of Applied Behavior Analysis, 32(2),* 175–83.

Wilder, D. A., Register, M., Register, S., Bajagic, V., Neidert, P. L., & Thompson, R. (2009). Functional analysis and treatment of rumination using fixed-time delivery of a flavor spray. *Journal of Applied Behavior Analysis, 42 (4),* 877–82

Appendices

Appendix A
Frequency Recording Data Sheet

Appendix B
Duration of Behavior Data Sheet

Appendix C
Latency to Behavior Data Sheet

Appendix D
Data Sheet for Measuring the Intensity
of Behavior

Appendix E
Time Sample Data Sheet

Appendix F
Permanent Products Data Sheet

Appendix G
A-B-C Data Sheet

Appendix H
Descriptive Analysis Data Sheet

Appendix I
Consent Form

Appendix J
AB Functional Analysis Data Sheet

Appendix K
Antecedent Manipulation Data Sheet

Appendix L
Functional Analysis Data Sheet

Appendix A   Frequency Recording Data Sheet

Behavior: _____

Definition of Behavior:

_____

_____

_____

_____

Date: _____
Observer: _____
Time Observation Starts: _____
Time Observation Ends: _____

Total Count of Behavior:

Rate of Behavior (if applicable): _____ per _____

Date: _____
Observer: _____
Time Observation Starts: _____
Time Observation Ends: _____

Total Count of Behavior:

Rate of Behavior (if applicable): _____ per _____

Date: _____
Observer: _____
Time Observation Starts: _____
Time Observation Ends: _____

Total Count of Behavior:

Rate of Behavior (if applicable): _____ per _____

Date: _____
Observer: _____
Time Observation Starts: _____
Time Observation Ends: _____

Total Count of Behavior:

Rate of Behavior (if applicable): _____ per _____

Appendix B   Duration of Behavior Data Sheet

Behavior: _____

Definition of Behavior:

_____

_____

_____

_____

_____

After each occurrence of the behavior, record the duration in the spaces provided below. If there are more than 20 occurrences of the behavior, use a second data sheet.

Date: _____
Observer: _____
Time Observation Starts: _____
Time Observation Ends: _____

Duration 1: _____
Duration 2: _____
Duration 3: _____
Duration 4: _____
Duration 5: _____
Duration 6: _____
Duration 7: _____
Duration 8: _____
Duration 9: _____
Duration 10: _____
Duration 11: _____
Duration 12: _____
Duration 13: _____
Duration 14: _____
Duration 15: _____
Duration 16: _____
Duration 17: _____
Duration 18: _____
Duration 19: _____
Duration 20: _____

Average or Total (circle one) Duration: _____
(To calculate *Average Duration*, add all of the durations together and divide by the number of occurrences of the behavior. To calculate *Total Duration*, add all of the durations together.)

Appendix C   Latency to Behavior Data Sheet

Behavior: _____

Definition of Behavior:

_____

_____

_____

_____

_____

Date: _____
Observer: _____
Time Observation Starts: _____
Time Observation Ends: _____

What was the activity or stimulus?	Latency to Behavior

Average or Total (circle one) Latency: _____
*(To calculate Average Latency, add all of the latencies together and divide by the number
of occurrences of the behavior. To calculate Total Latency, add all of the latencies together.)*

Appendix D Data Sheet for Measuring the Intensity of Behavior

Behavior: _____

Definition of Behavior:

_____

_____

_____

_____

_____

Date: _____
Observer: _____
Time Observation Starts: _____
Time Observation Ends: _____

Intensity Level Please write in the intensity levels for this behavior.	Frequency Please make a hash mark in the box for each occurrence of the behavior at this intensity level.	Total Please add the hash marks for each level and write the total here.	Rate Divide the total by the amount of time observed.

Appendix E   Time Sample Data Sheet

Behavior: _____

Definition of Behavior:

_____

_____

_____

_____

_____

Date: _____
Observer: _____
Time Observation Starts: _____
Time Observation Ends: _____
Observation Interval Length: _____
Circle which data collection procedure you are using:
          Partial Interval   Momentary Time Sample

Interval Number (If needed, write actual times next to interval number)	**Did the behavior occur...** ...at all if Partial Interval? ...at end of interval if Momentary Time Sample?	
1	Yes	No
2	Yes	No
3	Yes	No
4	Yes	No
5	Yes	No
6	Yes	No
7	Yes	No
8	Yes	No
9	Yes	No
10	Yes	No
11	Yes	No
12	Yes	No
13	Yes	No
14	Yes	No
15	Yes	No
16	Yes	No
17	Yes	No
18	Yes	No
19	Yes	No
20	Yes	No

(Use additional sheets if more than 20 intervals per observation.)

Total Number of "Yes": _____
(If applicable) Percent of Intervals in which behavior occurred: _____
("Total Yes" divided by "Total Yes" + "Total No" multiplied by 100.)

Appendix F   Permanent Products Data Sheet

Behavior: _____

Definition of Behavior:

_____

_____

_____

_____

_____

Product Measured: _____

Date: _____
Observer: _____
Time Observation Starts: _____
Time Observation Ends: _____
Total Count: _____
Rate of Behavior (if applicable): _____ per _____

Date: _____
Observer: _____
Time Observation Starts: _____
Time Observation Ends: _____
Total Count: _____
Rate of Behavior (if applicable): _____ per _____

Date: _____
Observer: _____
Time Observation Starts: _____
Time Observation Ends: _____
Total Count: _____
Rate of Behavior (if applicable): _____ per _____

Date: _____
Observer: _____
Time Observation Starts: _____
Time Observation Ends: _____
Total Count: _____
Rate of Behavior (if applicable): _____ per _____

Appendix G   A-B-C Data Sheet

Behavior: _____

Definition of Behavior:

_____

_____

_____

_____

_____

Date: _____

Observer: _____

Setting	Activity	Antecedent	Consequence	Possible function?

Possible Function 1: _____   Total Number of Occurrences: _____

Possible Function 2: _____   Total Number of Occurrences: _____

Possible Function 3: _____   Total Number of Occurrences: _____

Possible Function 4: _____   Total Number of Occurrences: _____

Possible Function 5: _____   Total Number of Occurrences: _____

Appendix H   Descriptive Analysis Data Sheet

Behavior: _____

Definition of Behavior:

_____

_____

_____

_____

Date: _____
Observer: _____
Observed with: _____

For each instance of the behavior, circle the letter(s) signifying which condition(s) were in place. Use the code below:
   D=Demand   L=Low Attention   R=Restricted Access   A=Alone

Instance of the behavior?	Conditions in place?				Write intensity or duration in this space, if applicable
1	D	L	R	A	
2	D	L	R	A	
3	D	L	R	A	
4	D	L	R	A	
5	D	L	R	A	
6	D	L	R	A	
7	D	L	R	A	
8	D	L	R	A	
9	D	L	R	A	
10	D	L	R	A	
11	D	L	R	A	
12	D	L	R	A	
13	D	L	R	A	
14	D	L	R	A	
15	D	L	R	A	
16	D	L	R	A	
17	D	L	R	A	
18	D	L	R	A	
19	D	L	R	A	
20	D	L	R	A	
Total Frequencies:					
Average frequency, duration, or intensity:					

Note: For interval data, use that data sheet in conjunction with this one.

Appendix I Consent Form

Dear Parents,

The staff at _____, would like to learn more about how to effectively manage your child's behavior. It appears necessary to conduct a functional assessment to determine the factors contributing to this behavior. To evaluate the factors maintaining the problem behavior, assessment methods such as descriptive and/or functional analyses may be used. The procedures we propose and all relevant information are attached. Because this intervention is a special one which necessitates systematic implementation, we require your informed consent before we proceed.

Please review the attached information regarding functional assessment procedures. If you have any questions or reservations about the implementation of the assessment, please contact us directly about your questions/concerns. We want you to be fully informed about the behavior, the factors contributing to its occurrence, and how we plan to intervene. If you are uncomfortable with this program, please do not sign this form. We invite you to discuss alternatives with your child's teacher and support staff. We will not proceed until we have your permission.

If you agree to the implementation of this assessment protocol and then wish to terminate the assessment, you simply have to notify us and we will comply with your request. The use of a consent form may seem very formal, but our purpose in using this written communication is to ensure that everyone involved with your child understands the assessment procedures and why we are using them.

If you have read the attached information and are willing to give consent to use the assessment described, please sign the program sheet where it asks for your signature(s).

OVERVIEW OF FUNCTIONAL ASSESSMENT PROCEDURES

Individuals with developmental disabilities often exhibit significant behavioral problems. These behavior problems include, but are not limited to, aggression, self-injurious behavior, property destruction, and self-stimulatory behavior. Accurate assessment is important for developing successful treatments for challenging behaviors. Individuals may engage in inappropriate behavior for a number of reasons, including to gain access to attention (from staff or peers), to gain access to preferred items, or to escape demand situations (i.e., work). In some cases, individuals may engage in inappropriate behavior to access the consequences that the response produces itself (i.e., self-stimulation). Functional assessments are used to determine the causes of the problem behavior and design effective treatments.

To accurately evaluate the factors maintaining problem behavior, a number of functional assessment procedures may be used. These procedures may include parent or teacher interviews, descriptive analyses, and functional analyses.

Interviews: Interviews are useful for getting detailed information about a student quickly. They also provide staff with valuable information regarding the antecedents (or "triggers") that cause problem behavior. Additionally, interviews can provide information about the consequences of problem behavior (i.e., how people react to it). Interviews are rarely used alone in the development of behavior programs given that the information is not always reliable (i.e., different reporters may have different interpretations of the same behavior) and is subject to bias (i.e., a reporter may say behavior problems are worse/better than they actually are based on recent events in the classroom).

Descriptive Analyses: Descriptive analyses provide a useful means for observing students and evaluating factors that may contribute to problem behavior. In descriptive analyses, a student is generally observed in his or her natural environment (i.e., school, home). Data are collected on the events that immediately precede (i.e., antecedents) and follow (i.e., consequences) inappropriate behavior. Descriptive analyses allow staff to collect objective data regarding the factors maintaining problem behavior. The opportunity to assess the problem behavior in its natural context and make decisions based on objective data can help staff make effective decisions regarding problem behavior. The main drawback in the use of descriptive analyses is the limited amount of control in evaluating the behavior (i.e., you are only an observer). Therefore, we can only develop hypotheses regarding possible causes.

Functional Analyses: Functional analyses are procedures used to identify the environmental contexts in which challenging behavior is likely and unlikely to occur. Similar to a descriptive analysis, functional analyses evaluate the antecedents and consequences that maintain problem behavior. Unlike descriptive analyses, functional analyses involve making systematic changes to the environment to evaluate the effects of different conditions on the problem behavior(s).

In a functional analysis, the student is exposed to situations that may or may not cause problem behavior. These situations include work/demand situations, situations in which social attention is briefly withheld (for one to ten minutes), situations in which preferred items are briefly withheld (for one to ten minutes), and free play conditions. Given the degree of control in a functional analysis, staff can accurately and reliably identify the consequences that reinforce and maintain problem behavior. Additionally, functional analyses provide a direct and immediate link between assessment and treatment. Adaptive replacement skills (e.g., using speech or sign language to communicate wants or needs) can easily be taught and evaluated in the context of a functional analysis. Functional analyses are extremely useful, but may be more labor intensive and time consuming.

I/We have read the above information on the implementation of a functional assessment for our child and are willing to give consent to use the assessment as described.

_____

Signature (Parent or Guardian)/Date

_____

Signature (Parent or Guardian)/Date

Appendix J   AB Functional Analysis Data Sheet

Time	Attention	No Attention	Access to Preferred Items and Activities	No Access to Preferred Items and Activities	Work	No Work
10 minutes						
10 minutes						
20 minutes						
10 minutes						
10 minutes						
10 minutes						

Appendix K   Antecedent Manipulation Data Sheet

Behavior: _____

Definition of Behavior:

_____

_____

_____

_____

Date:_____
Length of sessions: _____
Observer: _____
Observed with: _____

Define each condition here: _____

1)

2)

3)

4)

5)

6)

Condition	Session 1 Total	Session 2 Total	Session 3 Total	Overall Total
1)				
2)				
3)				
4)				
5)				
6)				
Which condition elicited the most target behaviors for each session?				

Appendix L Functional Analysis Data Sheet

	Series 1	Series 2	Series 3	Series 4	Series 5
Attention					
Tangible					
Demand					
Alone					
Play					

Index

A–B–C data, 84–88
A–B–C data sheet, 86, 139, 158
ABC quadrant analysis, 87–88
Abolishing operation, 16, 17
Access, restricted, 94. *See also* Objects and activities, preferred
Adolescents and adults with autism, 135–38
Aggression
  examples of, vii–viii, 4–5, 7, 41–42, 139, 144–45
  in adolescents or adults, 136
Alone/ignore condition, 98–99, 110. *See also* Automatic reinforcement behaviors
Alternative assessment models
  drawbacks of, 119–20
  functional analysis of precursor behavior, 108, 116
  functional analysis of requesting behavior, 109, 116–19
  reasons to use, 107–8
  latency–based functional analyses, 108, 113–16
  trial–based functional analyses, 108, 109–13, 119
Antecedent manipulations, 91–96, 102
Antecedents
  definition of, 19

examples of, 85
making changes to, 127
observing for, 84
types of, 20–21
Assessment of behavior. *See* Alternative assessment models, Descriptive analysis, Functional behavior assessment, Functional assessment
Attention
  addressing behaviors motivated by, 129–30
  as function of behavior, 24–25
  examples of seeking, 85, 88, 143–44
  received during time–out, 2–3
  testing hypotheses about, 93–94, 97, 109, 117
Autism spectrum disorders, people with
  communication difficulties of, 7
  involving in FBA process, 36–37
  restricted interests of, 9
  sensory sensitivities of, 26, 131
  social skills difficulties of, 8
  special considerations for adults, 135–38
Automatic reinforcement behaviors
  antecedents of, 127
  development of, 6

About the Authors

Beth Glasberg, Ph.D., BCBA-D, is the Director of Glasberg Behavioral Consulting Services, LLC, the Chief Clinical Officer of the Central Jersey Office of Brett DiNovi and Associates, LLC, and an adjunct professor at Rider University.

Robert H. LaRue, Ph.D., BCBA-D, is Clinical Associate Professor at Rutgers University and Director of Behavioral and Research Services at the Douglass Developmental Disabilities Center.